Twelve Alternatives to Time Out
Connected Discipline Tools for Raising Cooperative Children

ARIADNE BRILL
Founder of Positive Parenting Connection

Copyright

Requests for permission to copy, quote or excerpt should be addressed to:
Ariadne M. Brill
Email: info@positiveparentingconnection.net
Web site: http://positiveparentingconnection.net
Positive Parenting Connection
1st Publication , October 2014

Published By Positive Parenting Connection via CreateSpace
ISBN-13:
978-1502987624
ISBN-10:
1502987627

Disclaimer

Table of Contents

Part One

Introduction

Raising Capable, Confident, Cooperative Children

In my experience, it is how we treat children that directly impacts what they believe about themselves, and ultimately how they interact with the world around them. As a mother to three and a parenting educator, I have learned that a "discipline for obedience" approach that relies on Time Outs and punishments just doesn't give children the skills they need to be resilient and thrive. It is also an approach that often leaves parents exhausted, searching for answers and unable to fully enjoy their parenting journey.

Sharing ways you can, as a parent, model positive, healthy, kind and encouraging ways to influence and guide your child is the central idea behind this book. My intention is to support you to have the tools to parent in a way that leaves you and your child feeling capable and confident. While the most commonly known discipline methods focus strictly on managing bad behavior, the approach I am encouraging is different. It is not a method or a system of behavior management. Instead, it is an approach to discipline, which aims at keeping connection, cooperation and a dynamic parent-child relationship at its core.

As children grow, they make mistakes and act in immature and impulsive ways. Children temporarily forget what they should "know better", yet they don't do these things because they are bad. Children do them because they are still growing and learning. More than Time Out or being grounded, children need to have a parent willing to love, accept, forgive, encourage, trust and guide the way, each and every day. In working with families, I see over and over again how children thrive when they feel connected, confident and capable.

Children flourish when provided with ample opportunities to be curious, daring, compassionate, inquisitive, empathetic and creative. Children learn to be resilient, cooperative and emotionally intelligent when they are respected, involved, accepted, validated and listened to.

Recognizing and acknowledging that children are natural at experimenting and problem solving is central to the *connected discipline tools* and ideas presented in this book. My sincere wish is that the tools in this book will help you embrace how children learn and why what we perceive as misbehavior and mistakes are often a natural part of healthy growth and development.

In the first part of the book we will look at ways to encourage connection, set appropriate limits and how to foster cooperation. In the second half, you will find twelve tools for putting connected discipline principles into practice. These tools were chosen and developed based on real parent-child interactions, plus the most current understanding of childhood development, family psychology and research on parenting practices. Parent to parent, I can share that your child will not magically behave perfectly as a result of using the tools presented in this book. From toddlers to teens, children can be spirited, curious, determined and they will continuously test limits and make mistakes that call for daily guidance. What will hopefully happen is that these tools will create space for you to respond confidently to a variety of everyday parenting challenges.

The gist of this book? To give you concrete parenting tools and examples of how real parents are engaging in connected discipline, so you can choose how to incorporate connected discipline into your own parenting journey. While the parenting tools in this book are helpful for guiding children aged one to ten years, the self-regulation and problem solving skills you and your children will learn will be useful for life.

Discipline does not need to be harsh or managed by a timer. As I watch my children grow, I see that to encourage cooperation, at the heart of discipline, there must be mutual respect, trust, acceptance and loving guidance. Children welcome guidance when it is presented in a warm, caring and connected way. Children also trust boundaries that are set with kindness. While the connected discipline tools you will learn about in this book are peaceful and playful, they truly do have the potential to support you in raising children that are capable, confident and cooperative.

I wish you the best on your parenting journey.

Peace and Be Well.

"I doubt that we can ever successfully impose values or attitudes or behaviors on our children certainly not by threat, guilt, or punishment. But I do believe they can be induced through relationships where parents and children are growing together. Such relationships are, I believe, built on trust, example, talk, and caring."

Fred Rogers (1928-2003), Television Host, Educator, Minister, Songwriter

Better Behavior Without Punishment

Encouraging better behavior without punishment is not only possible, it is also more effective in the long run. This is especially true if you want to find a discipline and parenting approach for your family that will work from birth, through the transition to toddlerhood and continue to work well into the teen years.

Many parents believe that unacceptable behaviors like hitting, spitting, biting, teasing, back talking and frequent tantrums need to be managed with punishments. Time Out and taking away privileges are the most popular ways to punish children.[1] The authoritarian and punitive approach in the long run, however, tends to stop working and lead to more conflicts.[2] A recent study[3] even showed that most children misbehaved within 10 minutes of being punished with a slap or after being placed in Time Out.

While in the short term, a behavior we deem inappropriate or bad might stop with Time Out and other punishments, it simply doesn't help our children learn how to calm down, focus on possible solutions and make better choices. If you want your child to trust your guidance, she must feel connected, safe and loved, especially when she is feeling overwhelmed, tired, making mistakes, acting out, and needing your help.

Instead of focusing on learning or accepting your guidance, when punished, a child is more likely to:
- Shut down by looking away, freezing, refusing to answer.

- Feel ashamed, rejected, unloved.

- Get angry - possibly retaliating with physical aggression, spitting and biting.

- Be startled, cry or scream.

- Think about revenge or how to "get away with it next time."

- Withdraw by averting eyes, running away to hide.

- Become nervous, which may manifest in giggles, banging or throwing objects.

The big problem here is that when children are punished, when they feel bad or ashamed, the very part of their brain that is needed for learning how to behave better actually shuts down. You can think of that shut down as a disconnection from you. This disconnection leads to fear and mistrust and very often to thoughts of revenge. (If you were ever punished as a child, do recall feeling confused or angry about it? Did you ever think about how to get away with something or how to get even?) Punishment is actually the exact opposite of what children need when they misbehave. There is also a substantial body of research in the fields of psychology and childhood development that indicate punishment, particularly corporal punishment can have unintended negative effects[4] on children.

So what do children need to thrive and grow well? A review of seventy-seven studies[5] on parenting practices shows that the most important components for raising healthy, emotionally resilient, children are not related to punishment, or traditional discipline at all.

The actions parents can take to raise confident, capable, cooperative children are:
- communicating in a positive and calm manner.

- welcoming children to take an active role in problem solving.

- interacting with children on their level such as being playful and inquisitive.

- providing non-violent, guidance based discipline.

- reducing negative interactions such as criticism, shame and isolation.

- spending time together to strengthen the parent-child relationship.

The connected discipline tools you will find in the second part of the book were specifically chosen to bring in these very components of parenting, which are backed by research, into your daily parenting practices. Before we move on to that, here is just a little bit more on connected discipline practices.

Why Use Connected Discipline and not Time Out and Consequences?

When you observe "misbehavior" from your child and you intervene, what is that you would really like for your child to do? Do you want them to stop what they are doing? Do you also want them to learn something? Make a better choice in the future? Most parents answer this question by saying they are looking for a way for their child not only to stop, but to also be able to choose and learn how to behave in a different or better way. Time out most typically does not help children really learn to behave in a different or better way. Results parents may see from using Time Out or other punitive consequences are typically very short lived. The initial results you may see at the start of using Time Out, or after taking a favorite toy away, typically doesn't last long at all. For most parents, this means using Time Out over and over again and they often report that their child begins to act in a fearful, out of control or extra whiny way.

Using discipline tools that are intended to teach, like the 12 parenting tools presented in section two, sets both parents and children up for real learning to take place. The connected discipline tools in this book promote trust, respect, connection and cooperation. Each alternative to traditional punishments and Time Out looks to provide a learning opportunity, while still maintaining a thriving relationship with your child.

A connected approach to discipline also helps children learn the skills they need to be successful, resilient, happy, empathetic and well-adjusted for life.[6] The learning starts at a young age, but the results have the potential to last a life time. The skills your toddler will learn from problem solving with you now, are the same skill set they will take into preschool or play-dates and many years forward to deal with peers, friends and teachers.

If you consistently approach your child with these connected discipline principles in mind, as they grow they can learn to cooperate, problem solve and accept responsibility for their feelings. This guidance approach also helps children learn to manage their own emotions, like learning how to calm down instead of melt down, and thinking through their choices and behaviors.

It is important to keep in mind that all learning is a process. The 12 connected discipline tools are not as quick as counting 1,2,3 or placing a child in the corner. Just like it takes babies months to learn how to walk and talk, it will take practice, commitment and the willingness to try these alternatives more than one time to start seeing something you might call "results." Every new beginning or change comes with challenges. But using these tools as alternatives to Time Out, as well as other punishments and consequences, and making the time to work together with your child has the potential to:

- Honor your developing child's needs.

- Model the very qualities you wish to teach your child.

- Create more family harmony.

- Foster true cooperation.

- Encourage critical and creative thinking.

- Maintain a positive parent-child relationship.

Isn't Time Out an Alternative to Punishment?

What's so bad about sitting in a chair or a corner? You might be wondering if Time Out is really a punishment, or wondering how to explain to a family member why you are choosing not to use Time Out.

While Time Out was supposed to be used as a way to help children calm down and think about their actions, most children experience Time Out as a punishment.

> *"From a child's point of view, Time Out is definitely experienced as punishment...It is quite likely that children view this form of isolation as abandonment and loss of love." -Aletha Solter, Ph.D.*

If you find that when you use Time Out your child is running away, screaming, appears fearful, tries to hit you, is intent on escaping the Time Out spot or that you must use Time Out over and over again for the same misbehavior, your child is experiencing Time Out as punishment and Time Out is just not working.

The original Time Out was meant to give a child a break, a chance to step away from an overwhelming situation, which led him into unacceptable behavior. Time Out wasn't supposed to be about placing children on designated step stools and using timers and minute per year formulas. Unfortunately, the most popular way of using Time Out has turned what could have been a positive way to help a child into a punitive practice. Parents are much more likely to use Time Outs when they are angry, frustrated or annoyed. Time Out is also often used when children are overwhelmed with strong feelings or when a child refuses to "comply" with a request. Sitting in a corner, on a step stool, or being sent to stay in a room alone does not teach children how to behave better. It also does not help children learn to really express what they need in a polite or better way. As we reviewed earlier, quite the opposite happens to children when they feel isolated, afraid and overwhelmed. When children are afraid, they are not engaged in learning.

"Timeouts, while infinitely better than hitting, are just another version of punishment by banishment and humiliation. They leave kids alone to manage their tangled-up emotions, so they undermine emotional intelligence. They erode, rather than strengthening, your relationship with your child." –Laura Markham, Ph.D.

While Time Out may make your child stop a certain behavior in the moment, by itself it does not teach or help children to deal with big feelings, mistakes or the value of cooperation. It can also make children feel badly about themselves and so angry that they no longer want your guidance. What's more, when used all the time, this kind of interaction really can break trust and can hurt your relationship[7] with your child.

Is learning to step back, cool off and try again important for children? Absolutely, and all that can be accomplished with the connected discipline tools, without creating a sense of isolation or shame that too often accompanies Time Outs and other punishments. Before we jump into those tools, I want to first share these five principles for fostering connected discipline and raising cooperative children.

Fostering Connected Discipline

Five Principles for Fostering Connected Discipline

While the word discipline so often carries with it the implication of negative interactions and punishments, discipline really is about teaching and guidance. I have deliberately attached the words connected and discipline, in hopes that it will serve as a reminder of the positive power that heart-felt, thoughtful connection can have on teaching and guiding children.

When parents consciously make the time to guide with these five principles in mind, the effort translates into children that are generally kind, helpful, confident, securely attached, emotionally intelligent and resilient. It also means that your responses will start coming more intuitively even in new and challenging parenting situations. If you strive to follow these principles as they best fit with your family life, you will be actively respecting your child's developing needs as well as fostering more harmony and cooperation at home.

The five principles for fostering connected discipline are:

- Provide guidance that encourages learning.

- Allow the child to be part of the solution.

- Accept all feelings and emotions as valid.

- Lead with respect and unconditional love.

- Meet your child's needs (for rest, nutrition, belonging, attention, connection, play and discovery.)

Connect and Cooperation will follow.

When children feel connected, loved, respected and accepted, they will naturally behave well and turn to their parents for guidance. They will also feel safe enough to share their true feelings and be less likely to hold onto frustration and anger, which can spiral into difficult behaviors. Cooperation and good behavior flows when children and parents work together, instead of against each other. Conflict, power struggles, tantrums, and misbehavior often arise when the needs of parents and children are out of synch.

When children act in a way that we perceive as misbehavior, they are typically missing important information, feeling disconnected from their parent, hungry, tired, sleepy, feeling rushed, controlled, frustrated, discouraged, fearful or overwhelmed. These five principles for fostering connected discipline not only work to maintain connection, they give you the confidence to address any of these challenging moments as well.

Principle #1: Provide guidance that encourages learning.

Children struggle when they are expected to learn in a way that is not natural for them.[8] Playfulness, kindness, and opportunities to make mistakes are all ways that genuinely encourage learning and interest in children. As reviewed in the previous section, punishment and isolation really are not linked to real learning and don't promote the kind of security that children need.

When children feel capable and accepted, even if faced with a mistake, they will want to do better. It is important that, as a parent, you strive to offer guidance with learning in mind. Even when faced with conflict and stressful moments, if you strive to use clear communication, keep expectations appropriate to your child's age and ability, and interact in a sincere, whole-hearted manner, your child will be much more likely to calm down and accept your guidance.

Children are natural born experimenters and the more we allow children to take risks (with safety in mind) and investigate their surroundings, the more they will want to learn. Many children lose their natural inquisitive nature in the toddler years due to shame and pain-based interventions given in the name of discipline. Avoiding this kind of interaction and instead being deliberate with how you teach and provide boundaries will safeguard your child's innate desire to learn, discover, and explore. In your day-to-day interactions, this translates into creating age appropriate environments, childproofing your home, providing adequate (yet not hovering) supervision and providing calm, confident leadership when limits must be set.

Principle #2: Allow the child to be part of the solution.
Children are incredibly creative when they are trying to get their needs met. This often is said to be a "manipulative" trick. If parents encouraged children to channel that energy that is mistakenly called manipulation into a positive solution – one that is cooperative, helpful and in line with the families values – many conflicts would simply not happen.

When parents involve their child in the problem-solving process, the child feels accepted, valued and understood. Doing this also promotes creativity, wonder and cooperation. You will see that many of the alternatives to Time Out and consequences presented in the next section actively involve inviting the child to be part of the solution. Stories in the problem solving section illustrate just how clever children really are, and how simple solutions often can stop misbehaviors altogether.

Inviting children to be a part of the solution does not mean you must displace your calm, confident parental authority, or create a permissive dynamic in your family. Instead, it is about creating a practice of working together and encouraging your child to practice making good decisions. When children feel like they are part of the solution, they will also more readily accept and honor that responsibility. Even a very young child can come up with fantastic solutions to very complex problems. There are a few examples of this in tool #3 that illustrate this well.

Set limits and boundaries as appropriate, however, don't forget to allow your child to be part of solutions as often as possible. Engage your child with questions, allow them space to reflect and try to solve their own conflicts, listen earnestly to what they have to say. The more your child can practice and develop problem solving skills, even within necessary limitations, the more capable and confident they are likely to feel.

Principle #3: Accept all feelings and emotions as valid.
Children experience a host of feelings and emotions as they grow. Tantrums, hitting, kicking and whining are just some of the ways children may act out emotional overload. Children may also act out of bounds with joy, happiness, screeching, jumping and such. This is all normal stuff you can expect and learn to calmly respond to. Most of the work helping children calm down starts with accepting all of their emotions and feelings as valid.

One of the most important principles of parenting is that the feelings behind a child's behavior must be recognized, accepted, understood, and openly dealt with, before the behavior can change. –Jan Hunt, M.Sc., Director of The Natural Child Project

Accepting feelings and emotions doesn't mean you must justify any kind of behavior. An overly excited child shouldn't be allowed to pull a cat's tail or push a playmate, for instance. On the other hand, accepting that a child is afraid of shadows, even if there is no real danger, is important. When children are unsure or expressing their needs through misbehavior, children need parents to offer calm, empathetic, reassuring guidance. While Time Out typically teaches parents to ignore big, boisterous, annoying or "bad" behaviors, it is exactly when children are misbehaving and "acting out" that they especially need acceptance and empathy. Behind misbehavior like sassiness, defiance and rudeness is a communication of needs and a request for connection and guidance. Acceptance and acknowledgement of those feelings and emotions is the first step towards opening the door for the child to move through and beyond those feelings.

Just like adults, growing children tend to get frustrated, cry, disagree, have bad moods, and feel crabby and fearful. If we can, as parents, acknowledge for example when children are experiencing frustration or anger, we are helping our children develop emotional courage to feel and yet eventually overcome a host of different emotional moments.

Being emotionally available to your child, listening, accepting, validating and empathizing when they need that emotional support is not just important, it's vital. Every child in their lifetime will experience some form of failure, difficulty or challenges and hopefully a host of successes as well. You should not strive to keep your child happy all the time, or over-protect your child from negative experiences, instead, aim to simply accept where your child is and how he is feeling and guide him towards appropriate behaviors.

Limit behaviors, but do not invalidate feelings and emotional expressions. This is especially important if you wish for your child to be emotionally resilient and have the ability to self-regulate. For example, don't buy a toy or sweet just to avoid a tantrum. Strive not to tell a child when they have cried "enough" or insist that their fears are "nothing." Instead, recognize, validate and accept all expressions so your child can build a good emotional vocabulary. This support will help your child learn to manage his own reactions in various situations as he grows.

Many parents find it difficult to be fully present and comfortable with strong emotions. Listening to crying can be taxing and yes, often it is inconvenient. Even if it's difficult or uncomfortable, children's emotions need to be understood and validated so they will learn how to manage them. Even the emotions that come with misbehavior, defiance and disappointment need validation. Validation is not the same as allowing the misbehavior to continue. It's about making a sincere effort to listen and understand what is happening below the surface of that "bad" behavior. It is also taking a moment to set a limit with calm words – "I will not let you do that" or "I understand you really wanted that toy, and you are upset I did not buy it" – and then accepting that the child may dislike and protest that limitation.

Humans of all ages experience a wide range of emotions and no one person can be happy at all times. Some children, however, are more sensitive than others. They feel things more intensely and need a while longer to process disappointments and other strong emotions. If you find this to be true of your child or this principle challenging, there are three really wonderful books listed in the resource sections for more reading on emotional intelligence, learning how to emotion coach and understanding the developing child's brain.

Principle #4: Lead with respect and unconditional love.

Children learn to be respectful through their daily interactions with parents and caregivers. Unfortunately, parents do not typically give children the respect they demand in return. Parents often expect a lot when it comes to manners, sharing, kindness, empathy and forgiveness but forget to model these principles back. Children really do learn more from observing our actions than from the words of advice we greatly wish to share.

You can lead with respect when you listen to your child and show genuine interest in their point of view. When setting limits, be clear and kind at the same time. All of the connected discipline tools will serve to guide you in setting limits, but in general, do so with confidence and a calm demeanor. Remember, if you are confident in the limits you are setting, your leadership will be respected and your guidance accepted.

Don't allow your child to overstep boundaries repeatedly before addressing the problem. Setting limits early through calm, confident leadership sets the tone for inviting cooperation. Don't allow your child to overstep boundaries repeatedly before addressing the problem. Instead, be clear about what is acceptable; balance how often and why you are saying yes vs. no, and promptly set limits when necessary. Your calm yet confident presence and unconditional love will protect your relationship and influence with your child.

Additionally, demonstrate your unconditional love not only with words, but with your actions as well. Create small habits that allow your child to really see your unconditional love. For instance, hug your child when they make a mistake, cuddle them in the evening even if they were challenging at bedtime, smile when they enter the room, greet them with warmth when they return home from school, put your phone away when you are spending time together. Such deliberate practices really translate into a feeling of love and respect that connects and fosters cooperation.

Principle #5: Meet your child's needs.

For a child to grow and thrive, all of their basic needs must be met. Most parents consider nutrition, sleeping, clothing and affection when they think of basic needs. Attention, connection, safety, belonging, play and discovery are, however, just as important as affection, rest and nutrition. If a child's needs, both physical and emotional, are being met, they feel safe, loved and well.

When a child's needs are not being met, or they are having difficulties expressing their needs, they may become clingy, needy, whiny, confrontational, moody, anxious, fearful and combative. What we often call "acting out" behaviors, are typically indicators that the child has an unmet need. They may be tired, hungry, bored, feeling jealous of a sibling, needing more of a sense of connection or are simply scared and looking for more safety. Meeting a child's needs provides the foundation for good behavior because a sense of safety and security directly translates into more cooperation and acceptance of parental guidance.

"What makes a child's behavior misbehavior (bad behavior) is the perception that the behavior is, or might be, bad behavior for the adult. The "badness" of the behavior actually resides in the adult's mind, not the child's; the child in fact is doing what he or she chooses or needs to do to satisfy some need." -Dr. Thomas Gordon, author of Parent Effectiveness Training (P.E.T.) and founder of Gordon Training International

Attentive, respectful care is at the core of meeting a child's needs. While it may be natural to think about serving nutritious meals, providing seasonally appropriate clothing and schooling or learning opportunities, it is also vital that you invest in spending quality time with your child. This enables you to meet your child's needs for attention, connection, belonging, play and discovery. Laughing, being together and interacting in respectful ways builds trust. This time together also gives you important information you can use to better understand your child, how they relate to the world and what they are discovering. Striving to consider and meet your child's needs is the foundation for a good parent-child relationship and will help you and your child work together.

Making time to play together (distraction, cell phone and internet free) sends a powerful message to your child that they matter, they are important and loved. Meeting your child's needs will also preserve their sense of capability and support them as they grow. To promote connected discipline and reduce unwanted behaviors, aim to meet your child's basic needs, and, in addition, focus on providing ample opportunities to satisfy also the emotional needs of your child.

Summary
When your child misbehaves or makes a mistake, it is helpful to look beyond blame and shortcomings. As children grow, they make many mistakes, and they also need to learn so much

about regulating their emotions, and expressing feelings in socially acceptable and healthy ways. Misbehavior does not need to be met with punishment in order for a child to learn. Misbehaviors are opportunities to provide guidance, find solutions, validate feelings and show your unconditional love. Yes, you should set limits, and make your values clear, but aim to do that in a connected way. In offering guidance with care, your child will learn to trust you, trust their own capacity to overcome frustrations and upset feelings, and the true value of cooperation. This approach to discipline with connection at its core, will also encourage your child to learn how to respect you, himself and others.

"You can only create KINDNESS in kids by treating the child in a kindly manner.

You can only create RESPECT in kids by treating the child respectfully.

You can only create EMPATHY in kids by treating the child with compassion." –Dr. John Gottman

Part Two

Connected Discipline Tools

Connected Discipline Tool #1: Time In

Time In is somewhat similar to the original intent of Time Out. Time In is a connected discipline tool intended to give children a chance to calm down and reflect with parental support. The biggest difference is that children take Time In with a parent and not alone. There is no isolation in Time In and, when taken together, it is an opportunity for you to connect first, then listen, validate and empathize with your child. After your child has calmed down, you can then reflect together and, when needed, offer words of guidance.

The key to making Time In effective is to guide your child to take a Time In before a situation gets out of hand. This ties into the principle of leading with respect and unconditional love. Especially with young children, it will be important that you, as the parent, notice and observe signals that your child may be becoming overwhelmed, frustrated or ready to have a tantrum, strike out or melt down.
For example, if your child is having a difficult time, screaming or making unsafe choices like hitting a playmate or sibling, climbing unsafely, and so on, step in. Kindly remove them from the situation, do it confidently yet calmly and without reprimand, and find a quiet space to take a break together.

Let's Take a Time In: Using Reassuring Words
It may be helpful to some children to use reassuring words such as "Let's take a Time In" or "Please come with me for a moment" or "let's meet on the couch" to let your child know you need to take a break. For other children, it is helpful to use a gentle, physical touch such as a hand on the shoulder or arm in a kind yet clear way to guide your child away from a difficult situation. Mary shared this story on how she used Time In in

the park.

Matthew was at the park waiting for the swings. The other boy at the swings was taking a long time and being three, Matthew just didn't seem ready to wait any longer. I'm guessing it was frustration, but Matthew took off his shoe and threw it towards the swing. I wasn't fast enough to stop him, honestly I didn't really expect that to happen, but obviously now I had to do something about it. I walked over to Matthew and gently took his hand. He became upset and started to cry. I knelt down and told him we were going to sit on the bench together and he walked with me. He pulled a few times back towards the swing, so I reassured him he could get back to the swings after we sat together. On the bench, Matthew cried louder, and for a good six minutes straight. Honestly, it felt like forever, but I trusted that he needed to let his feelings flow. As he calmed a bit I asked him if waiting for a turn on the swings had taken too long and he nodded his head to say yes, and a big cry came out. I explained that feeling frustrated was understandable, that the other boy had been swinging, and swinging, and swinging for so, so, long! Matthew looked up at me and said "I sorry, mommy." I told Matthew I appreciated him knowing it was something to apologize about and we talked a few more minutes about apologizing to the boy on the swing. Matthew agreed it was important and asked for me to walk with him. We went back to the swings together to apologize and finally have a turn to swing.

Notice how Mary used gentle touch and eye contact to connect first in order to transition away from the area of conflict to a calm spot to take a Time In. Mary also remained calm, despite it taking a while for Matthew to calm down, which is quite typical of a child this age in such a situation. Sometimes these moments last a while, and finding the patience to be present really is all you can do. For many children, taking a Time In may become a ritual, something they look forward too when feeling overwhelmed. If you find a Time In is called for and your child walks with you and does not become upset, this is a good time to connect by simply sitting together, or, if you would like, you can also cuddle or hug. Next, ask how the child is doing, review with your child your expectations for the situation you are in such as not using hands for hitting, not ripping books and so on. When you feel your child is ready, let them return to the activity they were removed from. There isn't really a formula you must follow do to a Time In. Think of it as a moment to slow down, be together, and then move forward. How you choose to take a Time In with your child can be unique to your own needs. Serena's story shows well how to use Time In to address toddlers that are hitting playmates.

When Aiden was two years old he often hit his playmates at playgroup. No matter how often I told him "NO" or put him in Time Out, he just kept on hitting. I started using Time In with Aiden anytime I noticed he was getting frustrated in playgroup. I would let him know by saying "We're going to be together for a minute" and I would take him to one of the quieter rooms at the playgroup center. In my lap I would kiss him, gently tickle his arm and then let him know that hitting was not ok. He stopped hitting his playmates for the most part, and when he did hit, he started coming to me and pointing towards the other room for our quiet "Time In." Using Time In really made going to playgroup much nicer as I didn't feel like I had to say "no" and "stop hitting" all the time, with no change like before.

Crying and Time In
If your child cries or resists Time In, it can be helpful to remember that they are having a difficult time and need your calm, guiding presence to get through this moment. The crying and resistance is most typically not done to upset you, but rather because your child is upset themselves and overwhelmed with strong feelings. If you haven't used Time In before, it is possible your child may cry for a longer time then just five minutes.
Sometimes children store up negative feelings and once they start to let them out it's a bit of an avalanche. It can feel uncomfortable listening to your child cry. Acknowledging the

fact that your child is upset can be helpful. Speak softly, but don't really try to reason with your child until they have calmed down and take a few deep breaths yourself. During Time In, you may listen and support your child's need to cry, be upset or mad. While just sitting there and listening to your child cry may seem like nothing, your presence and care really is something invaluable. It means to your child that you are accepting and supporting them in an emotionally intense moment.

Additionally, by simply listening, instead of trying to eliminate that upset with distractions, you are also sending an important message to your child that you believe in their capacity to overcome big feelings like sadness and frustration. This gives them the emotional courage to face similar situations as they grow. Other alternatives, presented later, will also help you and your child work on emotional regulation.

As your child calms, strive to listen, empathize, reflect and validate feelings. With time, as your child grows, they will likely welcome this time together and use it to talk about their feelings and come up with solutions. Older children also benefit from Time In; you can see here how I used Time In with an eight year old child, Liana, that I regularly care for.

At the swimming pool, Liana decided to do some diving in an area of the pool that was very shallow. After the first time I observed this, I asked kindly that she find either a new swim move to do in that section or choose a deeper section in which to dive. Excited and bounding with energy, Liana worked on some new moves for a few minutes and then she proceeded to dive again in the shallow area.

The excitement of the pool and the urge to dive was making it really difficult for Liana to follow the pool safety rules. I told her calmly we would be stepping out of the pool together so we could talk. I acknowledged she was having lots of fun and let her know she could return to the pool soon and extended a hand so we could walk together.

We sat at the edge of the pool for about two minutes. First I asked if she was having fun and she told me about her favorite parts of the swimming pool. Then I asked if she knew why we were taking a little break. "Because I was diving in the shallow water." I told her that I cared about her and her health and that diving in the shallow water could really harm her. She asked if she could try again, this time where the water was right for diving.

We quickly talked about the water safety rules and she promised to follow them this time around. We were able to enjoy the pool for the rest of the afternoon and there was no more diving in the shallow water.

Just five minutes of connection, listening to what your child is feeling and talking about more appropriate choice really helps children learn about their choices and how to make different ones.

Connected Discipline Tool #2: Second Chances

Have you ever made a mistake and wished you would just have a chance to try again or start over? That is exactly what second chances are all about.

Children aren't born knowing what is right and wrong.
They do however have a drive to experiment, and are quite impulsive. This leads to many mistakes and many discoveries. For instance, when my son was two years old, he found some glue I had forgotten on the table after crafting. He opened it and basically painted the coffee table top with it. While I wasn't pleased with this situation, looking at things from his perspective, I realized that glue has an interesting texture. I also realized my son was really just investigating the glue, which I had left out in the first place, within his reach. To make my limits clear, but not take away his drive to learn, I explained that although it felt nice to play with, it wasn't ok to paint the table with glue. I offered him a second chance: "I can't let you put glue all over the table, do you want to try this again on paper?" He was very glad to make a paper and glue collage. When I wiped the table he also offered to help with the cleanup. On another day, he pointed to the glue and said "Only on paper. Only on paper."
Often what we believe to be misbehavior really is just the child trying to make sense of the world. Babies naturally pull, chew, mouth, smash and tug on things to explore texture, shapes and tastes. Toddlers like to open and shut, dump and dig. Preschoolers love to tinker and take things apart. For all children, natural curiosity and a desire to learn spans well into the teen years. Children of all ages also like to imitate, resist, exaggerate and experiment to see what information and feedback they will get from their parents. All that experimentation leads to mistakes and opportunities for do-overs.

Emma, age 7, had a habit of opening drawers and then slamming them shut. Her mother Cynthia shared that she believed the fact that someone always looked at her and yelled "Don't slam that!" made this extra interesting. Once she learned about this Second Chances idea, she started asking her daughter to re-open and close the drawer again more gently. She said something like "I'd like to give you a second chance to do that over again. Can you show me how you close that without banging it?" Cynthia shared that Emma actually learned in just a few consistent requests that she was going to stick to this whole second chances idea and the drawer slamming stopped.

Letting children have a second chance, sometimes even a third or fourth, or a total do-over, lets them recognize their mistake, address the problem and, hopefully, change their behavior. Children learn really well through repetition, and having the opportunity to do something again helps them remember what the better choice really is. There will be times when actually modeling the more appropriate choice will be necessary before giving that chance to do over.

Second chances are especially effective when a child has made a mistake because they did not have enough information. Often what appears to be defiance may simply be a child with insufficient information. Once a parent fills in that missing information, for example, glue is not paint or pulling the cat's tail hurts, the child can take a second chance and use that new information to correct their own behavior.

Encouraging Second Chances
When you observe unacceptable behavior using a second chance can be as simple as saying:
Would you like a do-over?
How about a second chance at that?
Other phrases to inspire second chances are:
I noticed you forgot the door open, could you go back and try again?
Seems like what you are doing isn't working, can you think of a

better way?

How about we start over?

Oops, this isn't going well, I think we need a fresh start!

Pause! I need a do over. How about you?

I can't let you [state unacceptable option] but I can offer you a second chance to [state the acceptable option] instead.

Modeling for your children how you make a mistake and start over is also a good idea.

This alternative to Time Out is great because it lets your child know you have faith in their ability to make better choices and fix their own mistakes. It's a very encouraging and validating approach as it helps children take ownership for their behavior, and reflect and accept your guidance. Second chances can even help children pause and re-adjust their attitude, like Becca uses it with her daughters:

Backtalk really bothers me, I want to raise my girls to appreciate the value of respect. I used to put them in Time Out for being sassy or using back talk but the problem wasn't stopping. With second chances, if they start back talking, I just say "Can you start over please and find a way to be respectful with your request?" I like this way of talking to them because I can stay calm, show them what respect is really about and still get my message to them in a clear way. The funny thing is that if I start talking in a way that isn't nice they sometimes will say to me "Hey mom, can we start over" which is great because while I don't want back talk, I do want my girls to stand up for themselves and be assertive when they are not being treated well.

Connected Discipline Tool #3: Problem Solving

What we see as a child misbehaving can often be the result of a problem that needs to be solved. Sometimes those problems push our buttons so much, we just can't focus on a solution.

Moira's mother, Marcy, was at her wits end because shoes were always scattered causing her and other family members to trip. No matter how much Marcy reminded and nagged Moira about the shoes being put away, she still found them everywhere. She decided to ask for her daughter's help to solve the shoe problem. To her total surprise, Moira suggested that they get a shoe rack so the shoes would have a "home." This solution was so simple, so obvious, but Marcy admits she was too frustrated about the scattered shoes to actually think about it herself. Scattered shoes are no longer an issue because since Moira asked for the rack, she has been really committed to using it.

Let's Think of Children as Creative, Not Manipulative

Children are quite creative when it comes to solving problems. Brainstorming together with your child to find possible solutions has not only the potential to solve problems and "misbehavior" but also helps children develop critical thinking skills. Problem solving with your child can start at a young age. While it's popular advice to not allow children to "manipulate" their parents, I invite you to reframe children's clever ways of getting what they want and see it as creative potential. This doesn't mean giving in to all demands, rather, acknowledging the potential for working together when appropriate and being willing to at least consider your child's point of view. Misbehavior and "manipulation" is often just mistaken communication. A child may be trying to say "I need more attention" or "I want to be part of this routine" and "Involve me, I am capable!" Unable to say what they are really feeling, children will invent all sorts of ways to get these message across, like whining, screaming, poking a sibling and so on. Sometimes problem solving is as easy as re-directing unwanted behaviors and creating better routines.

Each evening when Sammy's dad came home from work she yelled in excitement. It was just so loud and her parents really disliked the screaming, even if it was out of joy, because they couldn't talk to each other. Dianna, Sammy's mother, shared that no matter how often they explained and said "stop" and "no," the next day it would happen again. They felt out of options and tried placing Sammy in Time Out. "That pretty much ruined the rest of our evening with crying and Sammy refusing to sleep. We found your ideas on alternatives to Time Out for toddlers and tried to find some kind of solution." Dianna and her husband decided to try and find something else for Sammy to do and create a better routine. Their solution was to put Sammy in charge of putting the mail daddy brings home on the desk. Sammy now looks forward to her job and doesn't yell anymore.

As you can see, parents may need to find the solutions or suggest them for young children like Sammy, who was almost two when this happened. Yet, as children grow, they can participate quite actively in list making and brainstorming creative solutions.
The more you involve your child in the problem solving process, listen to their ideas, and welcome participation, the more likely they will be to try and honor the new solution. Problem solving can even help siblings resolve conflicts. Julianna shares her problem solving success story:

Noah (8 years) and Jonas (6 years) were having these awful fights every single morning when they had to share the bathroom. It was annoying to Julianna, and she felt like she had tried everything in the book to get them to stop. First she tried Time Out, then she bribed them with movie tickets. Then she took away toys. "Finally I threatened to cancel our camping trip. Yes, it was that bad!" Through coaching, Julianna learned about problem solving and decided to give it a try. In wanting to involve her sons in finding and owning the solution, they made a list of ideas together. Julianna wrote down everything the boys said, from painting walls different colors to installing laser beams. Yes, they suggested laser beams! Together, they went down the list to choose something that they thought might work. In the end, Noah and Jonas agreed on a schedule for who goes in to the bathroom first and a time limit for being in there. They even took a trip to the dollar store for a timer they bought with their own allowance (their idea, not mom's.) The solution the boys came up with eventually became their routine. When fights start up, Julianna tries to remind the boys of their agreement and things are much smoother now.

Using a sheet of paper or a problem solving notebook can be used for recording brainstorming ideas. Children really feel like their ideas matter if you take the time to write them down on paper (or type them up), read them together and then discuss which solutions may or may not work and why. By having several ideas and potential solutions written down, you can also revisit the list when needed and adjust your solution. While the process may seem initially long, the effort is well worth it because it not only develops important skills, it serves as a means to really connect before providing guidance and any needed instructions or corrections. With practice, problem solving may happen quickly and spontaneously as well.

As you introduce the idea of problem solving, it may be necessary to take the lead and suggest a few solutions (or implement solutions of your own such as child-proofing the home); however, with time, as children begin to focus on solutions and problem solving and take a more active role in this process, it is very important to listen to their suggestions earnestly.

Problem Solving Questions & Prompts

Problem solving questions can sound like:

- What's a different way for us to do this?
- I can't let you do _____. Can you think of a different way?
- Maybe we can find a good solution to this, do you have any ideas?
- Let's make a list of possible solutions, and figure this out together. What do you think will work?
- I'd love to know your ideas on how we can solve this. Can we chat about it?
- What else can you do?
- What is a different choice you can make?
- This seems to be a problem, can we try to find a solution together?
- What you are doing is not acceptable. Can you choose to do something else?
- Do you want to think of a solution for this problem? I would love to hear your ideas!
- What is a different way you can get what you want, without bothering your brother/sister?
- Would you like to make a list of ideas on how you can solve this problem?

Connected Discipline Tool #4: Asking Questions

Asking questions instead of nagging, demanding, assuming or insisting is an excellent way to model cooperative and caring communication. In the previous tool, we saw that asking questions can be an active part of problem solving. Asking questions is also an appropriate alternative to Time Out, particularly when you need to motivate your child to start an activity. Traditional discipline often focuses on getting children to stop things, for instance by counting to three or getting them to start something in return for a bribe or prize. Connecting first and asking questions can be an excellent tool for bypassing the traditional methods that often stop working unless you up the ante, i.e. make a bigger threat after the 1,2,3 or promise a bigger prize.

When your child is not cooperating with a request

When your child is not cooperating with a request, or is dawdling or doing something inappropriate, you can try asking questions that show interest and care to help them transition towards making a better choice. One morning, my daughter Bella, age 3 at the time, was throwing her baby dolls on the floor. The noise was bothersome and I worried her dolls might break. "Throwing your dolls isn't all right. Can you think of something you can throw around?" I asked her. Notice I did not ask her to stop throwing the dolls, and instead helped both of us focus on what could be changed. Bella looked at me and smiled, she took a pause then looked at her dolls. "The dolls hat. It's very soft. I will throw the hat!" Bella played throwing the hat for a while and didn't go back to throwing her dolls.

There are many instances when asking a question is helpful and appropriate. Let's take a look at some questions that foster connection and cooperation:
"So, what are you trying to do?" is a great alternative to "Oh, why would you do that!!!" because it helps you understand your

child's intentions and motivations and keeps the conversation positive and focused. Making an effort to really create some connection with your child, before making a request also gives you important information as to how they are feeling, what they are thinking and how you can best motivate and guide them in that moment.

"How can we work together?" is a great question to invite cooperation and diffuse a power struggle. Setting the tone with young children that you are willing to work with them and not for or against them, is typically very helpful in inviting positive interactions. Joy's mother shared a lovely story that illustrates just that:

My six year old Ronin and three year old Emma tend to dawdle in the morning time. I was so tired of having to nag them about each thing they need to do. Emma was landing in Time Out a lot and it wasn't working. I was nagging Ronin until I was blue in the face and he seemed to ignore me the more I told him what to do. Asking questions is now a great tool for us. Instead of nagging, if I find Ronin and Emma a bit off- track I just ask them "What do you still need to do before leaving?" or "How can I help you so we are on time?" I love how it puts them in charge of their own tasks, but the questions are enough of a reminder to get them moving again. Some mornings I need to be right by their side and sort of walk them through all the steps, but they are getting way better at it, especially if I remember not to nag.

One of my favorite questions is "What is something you can (eat/play with/do) instead?" Williams's mother has been using her version of this question to deal with conflicts with her son:

William is nine years old and he loves cookies. I had decided it was best for our family to limit sweets after dinner time, but sometimes this led to arguments. One evening he asked a few times about having a cookie. I really didn't feel like getting into an argument with him. I decided to just ask a few questions and give William some responsibility about this situation. I said to him "William, you know our family rules about cookies after dinner. If you are still hungry, what is something that you can eat?" This prompted William to look around the kitchen. He spotted some carrots and asked if he could have that instead. He made a great choice and we didn't argue about it, to me this was a huge win!

Moving away from nagging, shouting and commanding really shifts stress out of the daily routines. Striving to use questions will allow you to understand your child's intentions, work together and, when needed, offer a safe alternative.

Are there times when asking questions is not a good idea?
Yes. Sometimes, because of safety or time constraints, it may be necessary to avoid asking questions and simply offer your child instructions. There is nothing wrong with doing this, particularly if safety is a concern. I would not ask my young child *if* they want to hold my hand to cross the street or *if* they want to go to the doctor. There are certain decisions that are best left up to the parents to make and asking questions should not be seen as an invitation to permissiveness or to place undue responsibility on the child. For example, it's wise to avoid asking questions that are loaded with emotional responsibility such as "Do you want me to get mad?" or shaming questions "How stupid could you be?" Such a practice is unfair to the child and puts responsibility in the wrong place. Instead, asking questions is a tool to create dialogue when it is developmentally appropriate.

> If you are not ready for an authentic answer,
> don't ask a question.

If you rehearse the question in your mind and you are not actually open to accepting your child's authentic answer, then the situation does not call for offering choices or asking questions. For instance, if you must get groceries because you are running low on food and you can't leave your child at home alone, but you suspect they would rather not go shopping, don't ask "Shall we go to the store?" In such a case, try to frame the situation in a positive manner or simply explain that this is a decision that must be made by a parent. In that same example, it might sound like "We are heading to the store, you can bring a doll with you if you would like. Which doll will you bring along?"

While asking questions and giving choices is helpful to developing cooperation, it does not need to happen at every single interaction. It's all right to sometimes present information and not give choices; this happens particularly when you have more than one child and you are deciding to do something as a family. So long as there is a sufficient balance of opportunities for your child to participate, it's completely normal, realistic and healthy for you as the parent to take on decisions as necessary.

Questions that Motivate, Connect and Invite Cooperation
Motivating children to complete tasks, for example, getting ready for bedtime can be a fantastic opportunity to ask a question and place responsibility in the right hands: "What do you still need to do before getting into bed?" Such questions help children shift their focus to what needs to be done.

More questions that are very effective for motivating and inviting cooperation are:

- What do you still need to do before leaving for school/ going to your friend's house/starting that game?
- What is your plan so that all of your (homework/jobs/clean up) will be done before dinner?
- Where is a different place you could go to (jump) that is not the (sofa)?
- How can you and your brother work on that together?
- Let's try this again, can you show me your way?

- Can you think of a solution?

- Would you like to hear my idea?

- I would love to hear your ideas on how to fix this?

- Do you have any ideas you want to share?

- What if anything can I help you with?

- What would you like to do differently?

- What if we did this in a different way?

- How about we take turns?

- What will you do first pick up red block or blue block?

- Which part of homework are you starting with?

Asking questions and the pre-verbal child

For a pre-verbal child, it is also all right to ask questions as this is how you can start modeling cooperation. Your young child may not have words, but it is likely to answer you with a nod, pointing, frowning or smiling. Additionally, you can try asking questions to yourself when you observe challenging behaviors. For instance, you can ask yourself "what might my child be trying to learn by doing this?" Using your own question and observations may allow you to move in a positive direction and offer your child appropriate guidance for that situation.

Whatever you do, don't ask WHY!

Now, there is one question that might backfire. Young children rarely answer "WHY?" in a way that we expect them to. Their minds are naturally inquisitive, while we are already focused on very logical explanations. Generally, asking questions is a great approach, but if you only use the question "WHY?" you will probably not get the answer you want, unless you are willing to listen between the lines to understand your child's motivations. Questions that start with "Why" can also be perceived as criticism – "Why would you do that?", "Why did you not listen?", "Why do you do things like this?" If you ask yourself such a question, can you sense the potential criticism? Instead of *why*, focus on what can be done. I recall a time when my two year old was washing her hands, the water had been running for almost a minute and I really wanted it turned off. I was really tempted to just shut the water. Yet, knowing just how engaged and happy she was washing her hands and investigating the soap, I asked a few quick questions and offered information instead: "Are you enjoying washing your hands?" "YES!" "Well, the water has been running for a while. How about turning it off? Who is going to do it, me or you?" "I do it self!" came the answer and promptly, she turned off the water and moved onto drying her hands.

Would it have been faster to just say, "Shut off the water!" Well, faster possibly, but likely to disrupt her investigative process and lead to some tears of protest. This way, with three quick questions we stayed connected, she made her own decision and the water was turned off, which is what I wanted.

Beth had this story to share about asking questions:

My son Max used to roll his eyes at me when I nagged him about doing things. Now, if I ask questions that put him in charge of his own stuff, he actually does them. This tool has been a true life saver! It also works with my daughter Chloe and she is only three years old. It's probably my favorite parenting tool because it really works.

> Children are much more likely to respond to a request than they are to a command.

Asking questions is a great alternative to Time Out, nagging, yelling and engaging in a power struggle because children are much more likely to respond to a request than they are to a command. Commands often make children defensive and resistant instead of cooperative. Asking questions also teaches children responsibility and how to communicate what they want, need and wish for.

Connected Discipline Tool #5: Stories

Reading with children is most typically thought of as an activity to be done for literacy development and language acquisition. But books, stories and reading together can also provide parents and children with an engaging and rich way to approach discipline and emotional regulation.

Most children love listening to stories and looking at picture books. Listening to stories stimulates imagination, critical thinking and flexibility, and challenges in a positive way how a child is thinking and relating to the world. Reading together is also a constructive way to re-connect and direct your attention to your child when they are misbehaving as a mistaken way to have their needs for attention met.

Reading stories as an alternative to Time Out can be done in many different situations. Some children respond well to a parent that picks up a book and reads it out loud as a means to calm down from a tantrum. Jessie has two children and she has found this to be very true:

One morning my daughter Maddie (4 years old) was having a really difficult time. Everything I asked of her was just so hard and her standard answer was a big fat "no." After I gave her a few choices of what she could wear to preschool, she started to melt down and sob quite loudly. I asked her if she would like to listen to a story to help her calm down. She cried a few more minutes and then settled in my lap. We read one short story, and it took me not even five minutes to read it and Maddie was much calmer. Once she was calm, she jumped out of my lap, gave me a hug and said it was hard to go to preschool in the mornings. I let Maddie know I understood, and would also miss her and that we could read another story when we both returned home. After this short moment together, Maddie was much more cooperative about getting dressed, teeth brushed and shoes on. Reading a short book is a favorite go-to tool in our house for sure!

Helping Children Prepare for Different Life Events
Stories can illustrate problem solving, team work, and making amends, as well as many social situations like the first day of school, going to a doctor and why eating only dessert is not such a good idea. You can also use stories to talk to your child about really important subjects like the arrival of a sibling, good nutrition and how to handle being mad or sad. After reading such stories, your child may reveal what they are really feeling, thinking and deciding about these important subjects.
When it comes to encouraging good choices, it is also helpful to find and read books that are rich with feelings, conflicts and problem solving and then talk and reflect about the choices, feelings, and behaviors of the characters that were present in the book. When children can relate to the characters in the book, they are likely to want to either talk about their actions or model what they have listened to in the story.

When Behaviors are Repetitive and Annoying
If you are dealing with certain behaviors that are repetitive and annoying, telling or reading a story is also a very proactive way to avoid unacceptable behaviors escalating. For instance, if a child is beginning to use hitting or kicking to express frustration, fear, anger or other difficult feelings, search and add to your daily reading routine books with positive social-emotional stories, like "Hands are not for Hitting." These stories reinforce your message that such behaviors are not acceptable in a way that prevents nagging and lecturing. You can find a list of stories and books that help with social-emotional learning for many different topics in part three of this book.

Maryanne helped Ryan, age three, learn better coping skills for playgroups through stories. When Ryan was two, he started hitting his mom at playgroup whenever he was upset. He also started hitting his friends from playgroup, which was really upsetting to Maryanne. She started reading him stories like

Hands are not for Hitting and *No Hitting!* before nap and night time, mixed in with other books. The picture books made talks about not hitting not only fun for Maryanne and Ryan, but understandable and relatable. It offered a bridge into discussing this issue while also making limits clear. These reading moments also offered Maryanne and Ryan a chance to talk about what would be a safe alternative to hitting and soon enough Ryan started asking for help or a hug instead of hitting his friends. "We even have taken a break from play when Ryan was getting upset and read a book together. He calms down and talks to me about what he needs, for us this is a good, very good strategy, even now that he is five, it's still working."

Telling stories from your own childhood can also be a means to start an important conversation with your child. Particularly children between the ages of five and ten like to hear stories about what their parents did when they were around the same age. Adam shared this on how telling a personal story helped with bedtime:

One evening my son was misbehaving – well, he was refusing to go to bed and sleep. I was so tired, I really didn't want to start an argument. I remembered this idea about telling him a story so I told about how I didn't like going to bed because I used to worry I would miss out on something fun. You had to see his face, it just lit up and I realized in that moment that my son felt like I got it, I knew why he didn't want to sleep! He calmed down, got into bed and asked me to tell him more. I told him another story for five minutes or so and he fell asleep. Telling each other stories now has become a ritual and we both look forward to bedtime. What a difference this has made to us and our family.

For an older child that is already able to read alone, reading a book as a means to calm down is also a great alternative to Time Out. Sometimes children are simply overwhelmed and need a moment to calm on their own before re-joining an activity. You will see more ideas about dealing with this in the connected discipline tool number twelve as well.

Fostering Emotional Literacy

Creating a habit of reading not only fosters a love of literacy, it also allows you to re-connect with your child. The more connected children feel, the more cooperation and positive behaviors will naturally happen. If you include into your reading times an opportunity to talk about feelings, emotions and choices, you will also be teaching your child the vocabulary and knowledge they need to create self-regulating tools, like how to calm down before they melt down and how to assess their own feelings (understanding when they are mad, sad, glad, upset and so on) before acting. Such emotional regulation tools and emotional vocabulary will be useful as they grow and confront a variety of situations in life.

After Story Reflection Questions

Some questions you can ask when you are reading stories are:

- What was [character name] feeling?

- What mistakes did [character name] make?

- What could have [character] done differently?

- Have you ever felt like [character] did? What did you do about it?

- How was it for you, when you felt just like [character] did in the book?

- What do you think it's like to feel so sad/mad/happy?

- Is it ever a problem to feel like [character] did?

- Are there times when you feel like [character] but you aren't sure what to do?

- If you could change this story, what would happen instead?

- What do you think was [character] biggest wish?
- How did you feel when [character] did _____?
- What part of this book was funny/scary/weird/confusing?
- What part of the story made you worry/happy/mad/afraid?

While reading stories, notice how your child is observing the drawings and picking up on the different expressions that are illustrated. Talk to your child about what different expressions mean, such as frowning, smiling, crossing arms, squinting and grunting. Talk about any conflicts that characters may have with one another, wishes that characters have and goals that are being worked on in the story line. This kind of conversation builds a good social – emotional vocabulary that you can also return to later when offering your child guidance.

Beth-Anne shared this story about her daughter's difficulties with friendships in the second grade:

Mel was having a hard time with friends in the second grade, but didn't want to talk to me about it. It was hard to see her downright agonizing about her friends but not talking to me about it; it felt terrible. I had gotten some books at the library about making friendships but Mel wasn't interested in reading those. I think she felt badly that I was trying to teach her how to make friends but I felt out of ideas. We went to the library together and she spotted this book called *Enemy Pie* and wanted to take it home. She read it on her own and then later read it to me. The book is just genius about getting kids to open up how they feel about friends and enemies. It finally gave Mel and me a way to really talk about her friendship problems.

Connected Discipline Tool #6: Play

Through play, children can understand, experiment, try, fail, heal, triumph, create, wonder, thrive and fall in love with learning. Play can also be at the heart of effective discipline. Numerous researchers and theories have set out to explain the importance that pretend play has on the cognitive and social development of children. Play is much more than an outlet for energy or to keep busy. Pretend play and engaging in games that mimic real life situations are essential components of developing self-regulation[9] including how children learn to cope with strong emotions, not engage in aggressive behavior, develop patience, politeness, communication skills and empathy.

The Value of Play in Discipline

Parents at times underestimate the value of using play in discipline, because of the misconception that discipline should involves discomfort, shame or isolation. Effective discipline really can be play based. Especially because play is one of the most direct ways into a child's world. Play based discipline is very supportive of shaping, guiding and encouraging good behavior.

> *"Children learn as they play. Most importantly, in play children learn how to learn." Fred Donaldson PhD, play specialist.*

Playfulness and role-playing can be incorporated into discipline in many ways. Pretend play can be used to model good manners and to practice social-emotional skills such as taking turns, saying no politely and how to overcome conflict. Ensuring children have plenty of free and self-directed playtime also offers time for children to practice new and emerging skills.

When my oldest son Maxi was learning to get dressed, he was quite frustrated with buttons. Sometimes, this made him so frustrated he cried and refused to get dressed altogether. I found an old dress shirt from my husband with buttons and added it into my son's play area with the hopes it might serve as a means to practice this skill in a playful manner. When my son found this shirt, he decided to try it on. First he walked around the house announcing "Look at me, I'm a Dad! I'm going to work!" Then he was drawn to the many buttons on the shirt. I overheard him say, "I'm a Dad, I can do buttons!" a few times. My son sat for over thirty minutes, concentrated, pushing the buttons in and out of the button slots. He struggled at first, mumbling, sighing, trying over and over again, until it became much easier. The next day, when getting dressed, he chose a shirt that was also full of buttons and said, "I can do buttons!"

*"Play is our brain's favorite way of learning."-
Diane Ackerman*

Fostering Good Instead of Fixing the Bad
Fostering good behavior instead of fixing the bad is frequently more conducive to family harmony. Often this can be done using playful props and games. Puppets and dolls can come to life to teach positive lessons, ask important questions or infuse laughter into a challenging moment. Playful games can also foster emotional regulation and build a vocabulary of words that help children better describe how they are feeling.

We have a puppet at home named honey bear and he is great at helping our children clean up messes and giving them information for making different choices. I remember one morning when honey bear helped with a crayon mess – it went sort of like this: "I'm honey bear and oh it looks like you scribbled crayons on the ground, I'm flying to the kitchen to get a sponge for us to clean it up together. Come along!" After cleaning up together honey bear went on, "Oh now let's fetch some paper, will you color me a picnic on the paper? Paper is for coloring with crayons!"

The message was clear, crayons are for paper and messes need to be cleaned up, but none of this was scary or shaming. The children were really engaged and interested in what honey bear would be doing next. On another day they asked for honey bear to help clean up the playroom.

Heather shared this story on how she used a Teddy bear, storybooks and playfulness to help her older son stay busy in a positive way while she tended to her newborn:

After my second was born I had a hard time juggling bedtime for my toddler and baby at the same time. My toddler would get into trouble, or whine and it was not easy to deal with that and a baby crying. Our playful solution was that I gave him a teddy bear and some books and asked him if he could tell some stories to the bear while he waited for me to get baby ready for bed. He used to stay in his bed with teddy looking at books and I could take care of the baby. Later I used to pretend to talk to the teddy bear and the Teddy would tell me how much he liked the stories.

Play as a Way to Practice
Pretend play can be an engaging way to practice for real life situations like eating out at a restaurant, flying in an airplane, taking a bus or subway ride, getting a dental checkup, waiting in line and many more life occurrences.
Before we took an intercontinental flight, we set up a pretend airplane in our living room. My children at the time were two, four and six years old. With play boxes (pretend suitcases), we pretended to take off shoes for the security check and practiced using quiet voices in the plane. We played this a few times before the actual trip. The children did great on the plane, they knew what was expected and our flight, despite being over 9 hours long, was mostly enjoyable. When the two year old became a bit cranky, we reminded her of the plane game and how we were headed to a fun place for vacation. Talking about our playtime helped her calm down too and recall some of the fun things we would be doing once we got off the airplane.

In pretend play with your child, you can rehearse situations, and explain expectations in a way that children will really want to listen and follow. Later, when you and your child engage in these activities, they will know what to expect.

Sally sent me a note describing how she used pretend play restaurant to prepare her children for a big family luncheon she was really very nervous about:

I wanted to get Lauren (4 years) and Wesley (2 years) ready for a real restaurant experience, but I was feeling really nervous about it, knowing my whole family would be there and they'd be the only two small children. So we set up our dining room with a really pretty tablecloth, real silverware and glasses, just like they would find at the restaurant. I prepared a nice meal and we all pretended we were at the fancy restaurant. The children, my husband and I took turns pretending to be servers and we all spoke politely when ordering, plus we played games like I-Spy while waiting extra-long for our food to be ready. The real family luncheon went down without a hitch, my children knew what was expected, I remembered to bring them small toys too and we all had a really good time.

Don't Tickle Upsets Away

A word of caution about laughter and upset feelings. Sometimes, it can be tempting to make a sad child happy again through tickling, joking and playfulness. When using play to interact with your child, it is important to strive not to invalidate their feelings by using play as a distractor. Sadness, frustration and anger should not be tickled or mocked away. Such intense feelings arise for a reason, and while laughter is a very healing way to overcome such strong events, distraction and mocking is not advisable for optimal developmental outcomes. Instead strive to listen and accept your child's emotions and aim to use pretend play only to engage your child in learning, reflection, sharing her feelings and being part of a solution. When in doubt, honor your child by asking if they are ready and willing to engage in playfulness and respect their answer.

The imaginary worlds of pretend play are just as important for young children as the real world.

Sometimes children really like to be fully immersed into their world of pretend play. In this world, things may happen in a different fashion than what we adults expect. Cats may bark, zebras may drive, boats will fly and doctors give out candy and not medications. These play-based distortions of the adult concepts do not need to be corrected. In fact, most children bend the rules on purpose, knowing full well that they are inventing a different construct of the "normal" world. This is a sign of excellent social, emotional and cognitive development. Listen in, enjoy it, and honor it. Research supports that families with an atmosphere that welcomes and honors imagination fosters children that are more flexible, have longer attention spans, love to learn, and do well in their later academic pursuits.

Can discipline really be play based and effective?
There are endless ways in which you can incorporate play into your parenting routines - don't be afraid to be silly or funny, this will not devalue your parental authority. In fact, you may find that after laughing and engaging in play, your child will be more likely to accept your guidance.

I remember playing a game with all three of my children once which we called "The Magician Says!" except that it wasn't me making the magical orders, it was my children! I was asked to jump like a monkey, twirl like a ballerina, paint a silly picture, chop up apples and blow bubbles. We played this game for about an hour, and the children had to manage taking turns, and even worked together to create impossible tasks for me as a team of magicians with the powers to make mom look really very silly. That synergy of working and playing together really filled up everyone's attention and connection needs. Later that day, my two year old did not want to get out of the bath. I knelt down, smiled and said playfully "The Magician says everyone out of the tub!" and she laughed, stood up and reached her arms to me to be helped out. The game from before became a bridge for our evening routine and a way for us both to work together, avoiding a power struggle at the end of a long day.

If you are experiencing a lot of misbehavior from your child, don't dismiss play as a silly technique.

If you are experiencing a lot of misbehavior from your child, don't dismiss play as a silly technique. Seriously ask yourself how you can connect and enter into your child's world through play. Your whole-hearted, deliberate presence and willingness to giggle, play a board game, run around playing catch, fetch, baseball, shoot hoops, or whatever way your child loves to play can turn around misbehavior very quickly. If nothing else, it will give your child a sense of security and connection to you that will allow them to release upset feelings and then move forward and accept your guidance. This story from Janelle illustrates well the power of playfulness:

Corbin, at age 4 going on 5, would yell NO to everything I asked him to do. Put on shoes, get in the bath, get out of the bath, use the potty, eat dinner...I mean every single request was a big fat NO. Because of parent coaching, I started to notice that I really hadn't been focusing on Corbin's needs to have playtime together every day. Busy with work, I brushed him off and expected him to play on his own most of the day. I agreed to try building in playtimes for a few games, pretend play, wrestling and such just three times each day. Corbin became a new child. He looked forward to our time together and even though I was skeptical, he really did start saying yes to almost all requests. Things like bath and the potty became much easier to handle if I was willing to be humorous or playful. Now that Corbin is six, I don't have to sing potty songs anymore or play tag before getting shoes on, but I still make sure to check in with him and play a round of cards or something like that, two to three times a day. Putting more play into our relationship was just what we needed to end what I was seeing as him being defiant and difficult.

Connected Discipline Tool #7 Limited Choices

Offering limited choices creates a very healthy dynamic of interdependence between parents and children. Basically, it is a positive way to strike a balance between the needs and wants of the whole family. So often power struggles happen because what a parent expects and what a child is able to do in that moment clash. When parents offer limited choices they are actively working towards preventing power struggles and welcoming cooperation.

Limited Choices and Setting Limits

Offering a limited choice is also an opportunity to set limits in a way that is clear, yet kind. As we reviewed earlier, children are less likely to cooperate when they feel badly about themselves, so presenting limits and choices in a clear yet kind way is always more likely to encourage your child to work with you. Presenting your child with limited choices will also let your child keep a sense of control over their own lives. Kirsten and her daughter Isabella worked on this for a while:

Getting dressed in the morning can be quite the hassle for my daughter Isabella (six years old). She has a hard time looking at her closet and choosing what she wants to wear, which delays the rest of the family getting out the door. We used to argue, I used to hurry her up and then things got ugly fast. I felt like an out of control, threatening monster and I hated every minute of every morning. Learning to give limited choices with confidence changed all of that for us. Now if Isa is having a particularly difficult time, I let her know she has a few more minutes to choose or I will give her two choices of outfits to pick from. Sometimes she actually calls me and asks me to help her. Limiting her choices keeps us both on track in the morning and avoids me telling her she is going to school in pajamas, not watching TV for the week and sitting in Time Out for a year.

Limiting Choices To Foster Cooperation

Children thrive when they feel capable and trusted, and are much more likely to cooperate when they sense they have a say in what is going to affect them. While your child can't be in charge, offering choices, even if they are limited ones, is really important for maintaining positive self-esteem and creating a habit of working together. For Parker's parents, offering some limited choices while living with his grandmother was helpful to reduce family conflicts between all three generations:

Parker, at age four, was climbing up the furniture at his Nana's house, despite his parents asking him over and over not to do it. His Nana had also placed Parker in Time Out a few times because she really did not want her grandson to climb her antique furniture. Parker's mother Angie combined problem solving and limited choices to fix this situation. "Whenever I saw him start climbing, I gave him two choices, one was to play with the matchbox cars and the other one was to jump inside some hula-hoops that I would put on the floor for him." Parker would then choose the jumping or the cars, and eventually other play choices and he didn't try climbing the shelf or the sofas anymore.

When giving choices, it is important to clarify what the child is choosing and how that aligns with your family limits and boundaries.

Don't offer choices when you are not really able to honor them.

For instance, one family may not mind if a child wears rain boots on a sunny day. For another family this might not be an acceptable choice. Limited choices will work best if you only offer choices you are sure you are willing to honor and accept so you don't end up in another power struggle altogether.

Limited choices can be offered in various situations, from the daily routines of picking out what to wear and eat to choosing a time to do homework and cleaning up toys. Limited choices can also address misbehaviors by offering alternatives. For example, if your child is doing something completely unacceptable, try offering them two clear and limited alternative choices. These alternatives should be safe, respectful and acceptable, such as the ones Parker's parents were using. It might sound like "I can't let you climb the shelves, and we can either go outside and climb and slide OR you can try jumping on the trampoline. Which do you choose?" Another example might be "I understand you want candy, this isn't the time. You can have apple slices or some kiwi. Which do you prefer?"

Once the choices are presented, let the child choose what they will do and then move forward.

When Giving Choices is Just Not Working

From toddlers to teens, testing limits and choices is quite normal behavior. For some children, having to make a choice when they are overwhelmed, tired, sleepy or otherwise at the end of their rope simply does not work. For some children, choosing the option you never gave them, e.g. yelling "none" or stating a third choice altogether may happen. If giving choices is leading to more conflict, or a child refuses to take one of the acceptable choices you have presented, you may want to turn to another tool or set a limit. It may work well to try problem solving or taking a time in. If you sense it is a case of overwhelm and empty emotional reserves, let your child know that you will be choosing for them in that moment, and they can try choosing again another time. Your limitation on choices may be met with tears, in which case listening and validation are very helpful. Once the tears pass, offer guidance with kindness, such as suggesting a do over, or calmly restate the original two choices. If no choices can be made at all, calmly and confidently make the choice yourself and support your child in their frustration.

Connected Discipline Tool #8: Music and Dancing

When the music changes, so does the dance. -
African proverb

When tensions are running high in your house and needs and
wants are just not in sync, conflicts, nagging, demanding and
power struggles are bound to happen. Taking a quick but fun
break together to release some tension and connect one-on-one
or as a whole family can help both parents and children return
to feeling at ease and willing to work together.

How to Reset the Family Mood

Using music and dancing to reset the mood of the whole family
is a creative, fun, playful, yet effective move. What's more,
laughter, moving and music heal and promote a deeper
connection between you and your child.

A dance break is a beautiful way to repair from disconnection if
you are having an argument, conflict or tensions are running
high. Gena Kirby is the founder of Progressive Parenting Radio
and she has this very wonderful story about using music and
dance as an alternative to Time Out and consequences:

We discovered dance as an alternative to Time Out quite by
accident. I had given myself a Time Out when I become quite
aggravated over my kids' shenanigans, but instead of losing it, I
walked away. I went to the kitchen and started washing dishes
but first I put the stereo on. My favorite song came on and the
next thing I know I was dancing. My kids came in to say "sorry"
and saw me dancing, so they started too, soon we were all
laughing and singing and dancing and then we all forgot those
frustrating feelings. I love this solution. As parents we tend to
revert to the stressing behaviors we grew up with. I can
sometimes see myself model those behaviors and it scares me.
So, for me, the dance Time Out works on so many levels. I get to
be physical without hurting my kids. I get to model a behavior

that I don't mind them copying. So far it works for most meltdowns and arguments. Once we are all in a good place again, it makes it easier to talk about our feelings. I've heard the argument that unless you "discipline" your children, they will never learn. But that really isn't so.

A dance break all together can bring a whole lot of laughter into your day, diffuse meltdowns and even promote team work.

Engaging Children with Music
Aside from taking a dance break, music and dancing can be incorporated into many daily parenting routines. For very young children, singing a song to motivate and narrate what they are doing, such as a teeth brushing song, clean up song, getting dressed song, is often very helpful to reducing common toddler and preschool power struggles.

We used to sing lots of silly songs when my children were toddlers and did not like to brush teeth. One of my daughter's favorites was to the tune of the Brother John (Frère Jacques) song which we changed up a bit:
"Brushing, brushing. Brushing, brushing. Scrub, scrub, scrub. Scrub. Scrub, scrub. Your teeth are getting clean, your teeth are getting clean. Now you're done! Now you're done." Any song will do really, don't be afraid to make one up.

Using music to Energize or Calm Children
For elementary-aged children, listening to classical music during homework time can help children feel calmer and more focused. Did you know Einstein is said to have had many of his best ideas while daydreaming with music? If it's true I don't really know, but creating a positive atmosphere around homework with music sounds like something most children would enjoy very much.
Music can also be helpful to overcome night time and sleep problems. While screens should be avoided to guarantee good sleep, a yoga routine, an audio story or playing soothing, calming music in the background is a great way for children to

wind down before bedtime. Steve shared this lovely story with me about using music to soothe his preschooler in the evening:

Steve and his daughter Amanda, age four, were having a hard time with bedtime when her mother worked evenings. Amanda was getting out of her bed repeatedly and Steve, tired at the end of the day had little patience left after the fourth or fifth exit. In discussing some ways to create a more soothing routine, Steve thought music might work. So, one evening, Steve asked Amanda if she would like to listen to some music together, with the understanding that she would stay in her bed. After listening together to two songs, Amanda was visibly calmer, and ready to sleep. She asked if she could have two more songs, and by the fourth song Amanda was sleeping soundly. Listening to a few songs together has become a routine, one that creates a reason to be together, Amanda gets some special attention, but Steve can also relax after his long day.

Nighttime is not the only place for music and welcoming a calmer mood. Chiara, mother to two, often uses music to calm the mood in the family car:

One afternoon in the car, my two children were bickering and arguing, one of those typical, "don't touch me" sort of deals. Tempted to nag and yell, I took a few deep breaths and remembered I had my yoga CD with me. I turned the music on the car to one of my favorite yoga tracks that is very soothing yet energizing. The bickering between the girls completely stopped. It may sound weird, but it worked. The girls stopped fighting and eventually actually started to talk to one another in a not so rude way. By the time we were home, they were laughing and planning what to do together.

Music can also uplift the household mood and create a fun, energetic dynamic. Try a race against the music to clean up a room, or set up a fun playlist of songs for chore time and work together.

Joanne has used music to encourage her daughters to do chores around the house. Whenever her daughters, Sarah (9) and Brianna (11) don't want to do chores such as cleaning up their room or bathroom, instead of nagging them like she used to, she turns to music. Joanne likes to make an agreement with her daughters that involves some fun music and playlists. Once they decide on three to five songs the girls would like to hear, they then clean up for the five to ten minutes until those songs are over. This approach works well because it involves the children in the process, breaks the cleaning down into smaller chunks of time and keeps the chore fun. "Best of all, it keeps me from nagging about the cleaning up. It takes about three songs for their room to be all picked up and if we do it daily, even less."

June shared this story on how she ended hair brushing battles by using silly songs:

I sing songs for my 3-year-old daughter when we are brushing and combing her hair. She used to dislike it very much, but this way she knows when we will be done and we don't fight about it anymore. I make the song silly and say her name a lot and she knows I will brush only until the song is over. The music and singing her name makes her smile so much and the one song gives her predictability.

Many children also enjoy taking a music break as a positive way to take three to five minutes alone to calm down and reflect or dancing to release pent up energy. As a family, sharing musical moments can also build empathy and create a sense of belonging.

Connected Discipline Tool #9: Connected Consequences

Consequences, like taking away a privilege or grounding, are very likely the second most popular kind of parental tool used to control children's behaviors. Most parents use consequences as a means to address misbehavior. By giving a child a consequence, we as parents feel that something concrete was done about it. It's so easy to fall into the trap of thinking a consequence is necessary to learning. I'll admit to periodically falling into this trap too. Then I remind myself over and over again that the problem with consequences is much like Time Out; consequences are most often used in a punitive manner and are less likely to promote learning, connection and genuine cooperation.

Consequences That Actually Teach

Connected consequences are different in that when used properly, they help children learn to change unwanted or unacceptable behaviors. *Connected consequences* can also help children make better choices in the future while still letting them feel connected and accepted by their parent. While punitive consequences are determined by the parent and imposed at the moment of an infraction, *connected consequences* work differently. *Connected consequences* occur as a direct effect of the child's choice and must be related to the event in a teachable manner. Jane Nelson and Stephen Glenn, authors of the Positive Discipline series, have a really helpful explanation about consequences and how to keep them connected, fair and non-punitive. This checklist is a summary based on their work.

For a consequence to be considered connected, it needs to be:

- Respectful to both the parent and child.

- Related to the misbehavior or inappropriate choice.

- Reasonable as far as the child's age and abilities.

- Revealed in advance (or easily understood as a connected event).

- Repeated back to the parent to ensure understanding.

Connected consequences work very well in many situations. They can be used to encourage cooperation, problem solving and for helping children understand and accept responsibility for their choices.

Connected consequences are not always "natural" in that many natural consequences are unsafe for young children. Natural consequences should be allowed to happen, so long as these do not pose a danger to your child. For instances, consequences such as deliberately allowing a child to be burned by touching a hot stove, being hit by a vehicle for running into a street, or not having dinner because the food was yucky is unnecessary and harmful. Other natural consequences such as getting wet when refusing to take a rain jacket or having to get a late pass at school for not arriving on time would be, for many families, perfectly acceptable, however may not fall in line with your family values. Instead of prescribing what is acceptable or not as a consequence, I defer this to you as the parent. In deciding what kind of *connected consequences* to use, look for ways to connect actions and choices only to relatable, safe, non-punitive, age appropriate consequence that aligns well with your family values.

> A consequence does not need to be punitive at all. It can simply be "that which happens next."

How to Use Consequences in a Connected Way

Here are some examples from families, including my own, on how we have connected consequences in a non-punitive manner. For my family, as well as for Kerry's family, the connected consequence for a toddler spilling water would be for the parent and child to get a towel and dry up the spill, and then help the toddler place that towel in the laundry. Such a consequence is not punitive at all, it simply is "that which happens next." As the child learns to take responsibility for this spill, they also learn how to clean it up and will, as they grow, be able to accomplish the clean up without help.

A connected consequence for a preschooler that chooses to dump several books off a shelf can be to take the time to place them back on the shelf. A parent may need to stay close by, encourage and perhaps help a bit and also see that the child completes the clean up before beginning a different activity.

I remember a time when my middle son, Nicolas, was three. He decided to dump all the contents of his bookshelf onto the floor, producing a hefty pile of books. When he seemed about done entertaining himself with this pile, I thought it would be best for it to be cleaned up. I want my kids to respect their books and also create a habit of cleaning up whatever messes they create. I could tell the mess was too much for him to handle alone, but wanted to involve him in the clean-up process – after all, he had created that mess in the first place. Instead of talking about consequences, I simply said "do you want to use the kitchen tongs to get the books on the shelf or count them as they go on like we do when we play the sheep game?" His reply was filled with enthusiasm: "I can count them, watch me!" Around number seventeen, with a few skipped and reversed numbers along the way, he said, "I can't anymore" and was a bit whiny. I offered another choice: "Do you want to hand me just the small books and I will clean up the bigger books?" It took us maybe five minutes to finish the rest together as a team. The consequence in this case was taking the time to clean up the books, but to be age appropriate, I assisted in the cleanup since it was a pretty big job, and in doing so modeled how to take care of the books while avoiding a struggle or "battle of wills."

When in doubt whether a consequence is
connected or not, ask yourself if you are using

Teaching Responsibility and Life Skills
Connected consequences also work to teach responsibility and life skills, such as remembering to put clothes into a hamper so they get cleaned, placing toys away so they don't, for instance, get chewed up by the family dog or destroyed by bad weather. Ruth's story illustrates this well:

Ruth's son Jeremy, at age 9, had a habit of not placing his socks in the laundry area and instead throwing them under the bed. Ruth was tired of always nagging Jeremy to get them out from under the bed and into the laundry room. Ruth decided she would no longer ask or nag and instead told Jeremy that the only socks she would wash would be the ones she found in the laundry hamper and that she would not be buying new socks when the clean ones ran out. Ruth made sure to ask Jeremy if he had understood the new information about sock washing. Within one week, Jeremy was out of socks and became upset. Ruth asked Jeremy if he remembered what she had said about sock washing. Jeremy was angry and stormed off to school without socks and mumbling all sorts of horrible words under his breath. Ruth felt badly and a bit offended but decided to follow through with her part and did not wash any socks. To her delight, that evening, Ruth found a pile of socks in the laundry area. Jeremy not only apologized, he has since changed his habit to place socks in the laundry right away.

When in doubt whether a consequence is connected or not, ask yourself if you are using a consequence to help your child learn or just to show them you are in charge. If your intent is to help your child learn and you find the criteria for a connected consequence has been met, then you are using consequences in a positive and helpful manner. Andrea shared a story about her son Kyle that really illustrates how she stuck with connected consequences, asking questions and validation to guide her son on making better choices about toy clean up and screen time:

My son Kyle, 10 years old, had dumped pretty much every toy he owned on the floor of his room during playtime. The day was almost over so I asked him to clean up his room. He really didn't want to clean his toys and asked instead to use the computer. I explained to Kyle he would need to clean up before any screen time. He was not happy about that at all and actually kicked around yet another bin with dinosaurs, making his mess even bigger. Kyle pouted for a few minutes, and was visibly annoyed. I said to him "you seem quite annoyed with this" and he confessed the mess was just too much for him. I asked him what part of the room he could start with and periodically visited him to encourage him in the process. About thirty minutes later he was finished and it was dinnertime, so there was no time to play on the computer. Kyle was quite upset about missing screen time that day, but ever since he has never dumped out every toy and instead he has been more careful about just how many toys to have out at once.

Connected Consequences and Crying
Just because a consequence is connected to what the child did, does not mean they will readily want to accept that consequence. When facing the possibility of a consequence, even if connected and set well in advance, a child may refuse, cry, and become frustrated or angry about the fact that you are following through with the agreed upon consequence. In such a situation, it is important to validate and empathize with the child's feelings while still following through with that consequence in a kind and clear manner. You may need to combine other tools such as Tool #12, the Calm Down Plan or Tool #1, Time In, if this happens often.

While it's at times difficult or even sad to see our children upset or frustrated, it is important to not rescue your child all the time from connected consequences. Connected consequences are truly excellent learning moments. Instead of preventing all disappointments, aim to be present and supportive when your child experiences a difficult moment as a result of their choices.

Why do children refuse consequences, even if presented in a calm and connected way?

A child may be overwhelmed, unmotivated or simply unable to accept a consequence at that time that it happens. Even if a child believes the consequence is fair, they still might not really accept it. If you have ever received a speeding ticket, ate too much dessert or had to pay a late fee, you might relate to that feeling. Sometimes, even if we know better and know there is a potential consequence, we choose badly anyway. Particularly for young children, this resistance to consequences is developmentally appropriate. Personally, I find it best to not focus on blame or "I told you so" and instead take a moment to empathize and validate. After that, keep your calm and follow through or allow the connected consequence to be the only "teacher."

Thinking back to the initial five principles, this is again a case where providing calm leadership and trusting your child's ability to feel and eventually overcome big feelings and provide unconditional love at this time becomes very important.

Connected Discipline Tool #10: Just Breathe

No matter how pro-actively and calmly you intend to approach parenting and discipline, there will be times when you are likely to feel stressed, overwhelmed, tired, scared, mad, grumpy or annoyed. The same can be said about children. It's simply not fair to expect that children will have perfect days and great moods all the time. Adults and children alike experience a host of emotions on an ongoing basis and sometimes, no matter what your age, it can seem overwhelming to manage it all. Chances are, your child has at some point cried about something like picking up toys, getting buckled into the car seat or having to stop a really fun activity. Maybe, they have whined about something they disliked, such as a meal, sharing toys, wanting more allowance, having to go to an appointment or having to wait a long time for something. While it is developmentally expected that feeling overwhelmed, fear and tiredness may manifest in tantrums, whining and even aggression, children can also be supported to develop better and more appropriate coping skills that make these situations much easier for the whole family.

When my daughter was three, we avoided what could have been a big meltdown at the supermarket by combining breathing, asking questions and validation.

"Can we get this, mama?" Bella said at the check-out.
"That looks beautiful, Bella, so sparkly. Today, I am not buying that bracelet."
"I sooo love it!" she said and I saw her tense up and a few tears welling up in her eyes. I tried to think about the situation from her perspective.
At age three, that sparkling bracelet right at eye level was really tempting her. I knelt down and said, "You wish I would buy that for you. Do you find it pretty and sparkly?" She replied that she really did want it.

"I believe you" I offered "And today, my answer is no. Would you like to take a few deep breaths and have hug?" We took a few big breaths together, and I offered Bella a big hug. "I know you really want the bracelet, and today I am not buying it." I repeated. "Ok Mama." She replied. We left the store and in the car on the way home she said, "I'm taking more breaths, about the bracelet." Which I understood was her way of telling me she was still upset about it and needed to talk more about leaving the pretty bracelet at the store. We talked about it some more, and I used words like "disappointed", "hopeful" and "upset" to help her built her emotional vocabulary. Finally, she took an exaggeratedly big breath and asked if I could remember the bracelet for a special day like her birthday in a few months. Taking deep breaths through this situation helped us both remain calm and connected to one another.

Learning to Calm Down Instead of Melting Down

For young children, learning to calm down instead of melting down takes practice, encouragement and emotional coaching. It's quite popular advice to dismiss children's wishes, ignore them and then eventually place children that are having a tantrum as a result of their frustration into Time Out. The problem is that for a child to sit alone, in a corner, during this time of really strong emotions, triggers their brain to feel even more overwhelmed and scared. Time Out can't teach children to regulate their emotions. Parents, however, that take the time and care to support their child as they experience this intense emotional overload, can not only teach a child to regulate their emotions, they send a very powerful message of unconditional love. Amy Phoenix is a mother to five children and the author of Presence Parenting. Her story here shows how she uses breathing to find calm and reconnect with her children:

Changing the way I (Amy) respond to my children when they or I feel upset has been a process. One of the most helpful tools we are integrating is noticing our breath and bodies. Often when we're upset we're not paying attention to our bodies very much and it can be really helpful to do so. While all of our kids benefit from taking a moment to breathe (and I do also), recently my two and three year olds have been willing to stop in the tracks of anger, take a deep and relaxing breath and then start again. One time my three year old was gritting her teeth, almost ready to throw a toy, and as I went over to her I breathed deeply myself. Then I gently placed my hand in the middle of her back and asked if she wanted to take a deep breath with me. She did, instantly, and it allowed enough space for us to talk through the upset so she could do something more appropriate with the anger (like talk about how she feels and what she needs). Learning and sharing these skills continually changes my life - and the lives of my children. Even though there are challenges, I'm coming to realize I can navigate them with the strengths I have inside - starting with the ability to notice my breath and body. It feels amazing to share these simple experiences with the kids and know that they will benefit them for their whole lives.

Four Ways to Introduce Breath Awareness to your Child

Most children learn well how to focus on their breath by following a parent's example and playing breathing games, so below you will find four ways to introduce breath awareness to your child. It will be most helpful to your child to learn these breathing games when they are calm, this way they can recall the skills when they need them most, such as a time of distress, when they're overwhelmed or tiredness.

Blowing bubbles

Most children love playing with bubbles and, aside from being fun, it is also a great breathing regulation game. Learning to blow soap from a bubble wand to create small, medium and large bubbles is very helpful to learn how to control the power of our breath. Invite your child to blow bubbles and tell you how much air and breaths they needed to get bubbles to come out. Try small, tiny breaths, fast, slow, long, deep and even funny breaths and see how the bubbles come out.

Candle Control

Sit with your child in a dimmed room in front of one or a few candles and watch the flame flicker. Keep a lighter nearby to reset the candles as needed. Take a few deep breaths together as you watch the candle sway. Invite your child to use long, calm breaths through her mouth to move the flame, yet at the same time trying not to let it turn off the flame. Invite your child to take several short, quick breaths through her mouth, again, being careful not to let the candle get blown off. Alternate between long and short breaths. Finally let your child take a big, strong breath that turns the candle off. Repeat as you would like. Please use caution and your best judgment as this breathing exercise uses real candles and fire.

Flower and a Candle

This is a pretend play game that helps children learn about breathing, I have seen several versions of this game, so here I will share how I play this game with my children and in playgroups that I facilitate. You can use props if available such as a play flower and a candle, or simply invite your child to imagine the flower and the candle. First, your child takes a deep breath through the nose, like they are smelling a flower. Invite your child to hold their breath for two to three seconds. Then they can release their breath through their mouth as if they were blowing out a candle. Repeat three to five times. To include some emotion coaching into this game, you may invite your child to think about happy, joyful, positive thoughts as they inhale (smelling the flower) and to think about negative, overwhelming, stressful thoughts leaving their minds as they exhale (blow the candle).

Bunny & Lion's Breaths

Teaching children to breathe like animals combines pretend play, breathing and emotional regulation all into one package. For all my children, reminding them to take three small bunny breaths has always helped them stop whining and reconnect with me and make requests in a clear voice. Lion roars can help a child exhale pent up frustration well before it turns into a tantrum, meltdown or power struggle. Introduce this game as a way to teach your child different ways of breathing that show variation in the depth and length of the breath. Short, rhythmic breaths saying "he, he, he" are energizing, long roar like breaths are tension relieving. You can add on jumping and exhaling like a frog, moving the whole body like an elephant etc. to introduce the idea of working together (parent and child) to focus breathing.

Breathing To Deal with Whining, Back Talk and Power Struggles
Focused breathing is a great way to deal with whining, tantrums, power struggles and back talking. This story from Cristina is a good example:

Cristina's daughter Nayla is six years old and used to get really whiny and overwhelmed when running errands together with her mother. Cristina had tried many tricks like distracting with treats and snacks, bringing stickers along or promising Nayla a prize for "good" behavior. Nothing seemed to help Nayla cope with even a thirty minute trip to the store or post office. Full blown meltdowns started making Cristina dread outings and felt resentful. After Cristina introduced the idea of animal breaths to Nayla in a playful manner, she started to pause between errands and play a short round of Lion roaring or Giraffe long, deep breaths to help Nayla calm and renew her energy and focus for the next stop. Within a few weeks' time, Nayla started taking these breaths on her own, when standing around waiting for her mother. Cristina shared that Nayla now is much more willing to go on errands and she no longer has to brace for huge meltdowns once they return to the car or home. Taking a moment to practice breaths also helped mother and daughter take a moment to connect and be together in between errands, making this a win-win solution for the family.

One of the best coping skills there is for teaching children how not to melt down (a.k.a. have a huge tantrum mid grocery store) is by helping children learn to focus on their breathing. No matter how young or old, breathing exercises can be a helpful way to deal with anxiety, anger and being overwhelmed. Children as young as one year old, can learn how to pay attention to their breathing in ways that will help reduce, and eventually prevent, meltdowns, tantrums and whining.

Learning focused breathing is also an important skill for parents that wish to offer connected discipline. When you feel challenged by your child's behaviors and choices, it may be helpful to remind yourself to pause and breathe before making any decisions.

"Stop. Slow down and consciously breathe out stress." Genevieve Simperingham, Mother and Founder of the Peaceful Parent Institute.

Connected Discipline Tool #11: Start with Art

Many children enjoy painting, coloring and drawing. Using art as a gateway to reflection can be a positive and encouraging way for children to talk about their feelings, actions and choices. An added benefit of introducing art into your discipline and parenting routines is that children whose creativity is nurtured are curious and feel inspired to learn.

Art can be a facilitator of emotional intelligence because it serves as a way for children to document and translate their feelings.

Art is so much more than developing interesting color combinations, drawing or painting. Art can be a facilitator of emotional intelligence because it serves as a way for children to document and translate their feelings in a way you can see, discuss and understand. Through art, children can also explore multiple solutions to any one problem and actively work on open-ended thinking. Creating art is an active and engaged way for children to take risks, grow from mistakes and strengthen their attention spans. Art can also open the door to important conversations and life lessons.

One afternoon, at the park, my then four-year-old son ran with some friends towards a fence behind some trees. Just moment later I heard some laughter and all the boys ran back. Curious, I asked my son what they were playing and my son said "oh nothing!" The running, the yelling and laughter happened again. From the boys faces I could tell something was going on. I knelt down and looked at my son's sparkly face.
Half smiling, my son first said, "I didn't do anything. It was that boy!" but his friend insisted that my son had thrown some rocks at cars. My son kept saying he hadn't done a thing so I

repeated his story back to him. "So you were running to the fence, then you did nothing and you ran back. Is that right?" Almost immediately tears welled up in his sweet face and he told me he and the other boys had thrown some rocks over the fence and it was "so cool!", but they had almost hit a passing car so they ran away.

In that moment, my mind filled with terrible scenarios, windshields breaking, cars crashing, drivers being hurt, I felt my whole body tense up. It's amazing how much fear can well up so quickly when it comes to parenting! I counted slowly to ten, trying to decide how I could respond in a way that would be compassionate, gentle but with the intent to help my son realize he had made a mistake and that lying really wasn't all right either.

I didn't feel like it was appropriate to drag out the conversation at the park, I didn't want to rush the process and the drivers of the passing cars were long gone anyways and thankfully not harmed. I calmly told my son that it was almost time for dinner, that he could play on the playground area but to please stay away from the fence for now. Then I added quietly "Let's make a picture about what happened when we get home, all right? Then we can talk about it and make a plan." My son replied happily that he would stay where I could see him and after I helped my daughter on the swings for a few minutes we headed home.

At home, my son pulled out a set of markers and a sheet of paper. He started drawing the park, his friends, the passing cars and rocks flying in the air. When he was finished drawing, we looked at the picture together and I asked some questions that I hoped would help him make a connection and spark some reflection.

I asked if he remembered the hailstorm we had had a few months prior and what the ice rocks had done to our car. He remembered and said that the big ice chunks had dented the whole car and broken some glass in the garden. Next I asked if he could imagine if rocks were raining from the sky how that would look. This he found intriguing but soon decided that people or things could get hurt, just like with the hail. Finally I asked what he thought about what he had decided to do at the park with the rocks. His smile vanished and he looked at me very seriously. "I could have hurt someone or broken their car. It wasn't a good choice even though it was fun when we did it. I'm really sorry to that person," he said. "I'm not going to throw rocks ever again. Or can I throw them into the river? If I make sure nobody can get hurt? Not even a turtle or a frog in sight, and then it's OK, right? Oh and I am really sorry I said it wasn't me, because it was, I did it and I'm sorry."

In this process, I know my son came out feeling genuinely sorry, for denying what he did and for throwing the rocks. What I also know is that we both walked away from this experience connected, and with our relationship strengthened, not torn.

Helping Children Tell Their Stories

Art is a wonderful way for children to tell their stories. When children tell their stories, they process their emotions, feelings and the events that are central to their development. Children are bound to experience moments of joy, sadness, frustration, bewilderment and many more as they grow and develop. Children that hold on to upsetting events instead of sharing them, tend to act out those feelings through whining, crying, defiance and back-talking. When children can instead tell their stories through art or some other way, they can make sense of their world, learn about themselves, feel better and find the emotional courage to move through their feelings and then forward.

"Sometimes parents avoid talking about upsetting experiences, thinking that doing so will reinforce their children's pain or make things worse. Actually, telling the story is often exactly what children need, both to make sense of the event and to move on to a place where they can feel better about what happened."
Daniel J. Siegel, M.D. and Tina Payne Bryson, PH.D.

Suggestions on how to include art into your parenting and discipline routines:

- Encourage your child to draw a picture for someone as a means to make amends.
- Invite your child to paint or draw her feelings when she is very upset.
- Create drawings with your child of faces with various expressions and use these to talk about feelings and emotions.
- Keep an art journal in which your child can create and record memories and important thoughts.
- Decorate your family rules with art work from every member of the family.
- Encourage your child to make a picture about any event they may be anxious, excited or worried about.
- Create pictures or drawings of your child's daily routines as a visual way to remind your child of her responsibilities.
- Invite your child to draw or create something to process and honor the loss of a family member or beloved pet.
- Use pictures as ways to say thank you to family members or friends for presents, outings and special gatherings.
- Cover one wall in the home with paper so the children

may color it and decorate it when they are bored, happy, creative, upset, overwhelmed, etc.

- Create a habit of giving each other small pictures or drawings to exchange appreciations.
- Set time aside each week to create art together as a means to connect and spend time together.
- Bring coloring pencils and paper with you when your child must wait such as doctor visits, restaurants, post office, etc.
- Invite your child to draw and color pictures about his life, staple many together as a homemade "All about Me" booklet.

Make Time to Listen

When working at my desk, I often invite my daughter to sit near me with her crayons and blank sheets of paper. She uses this time to make many pictures and I take several breaks to listen to her stories about flowers, mountain, houses, dogs and rocket ships. Often making the time to listen to her talk about these drawings created another hour or so for me of uninterrupted working time. When children spend time creating and then sharing thoughts about their work, they actively engage their senses, develop their attention span and refuel their attention needs by talking about their creations. Adding creativity and art work into your parenting practice, particularly when followed up with the story telling process, is very good for emotional development, as well as a means to create more connection between you and your child. Making time to listen also builds trust and this willingness to listen earnestly to your child will serve you well, particularly as your child grows and their experiences become more and more complex. Talking about the pretty flowers and rainbows today, or throwing rocks, opens the door to talking about feeling left out in school, the bullies, saying no to drugs, sexual education, cheating, stealing, honesty and so on. Keep that door open because it's well worth it.

Connected Discipline Tool #12: Calm Down Plan

Helping both parents and children to learn to calm down and confront challenges and misbehaviors with a clear mind was the original intent of Time Out. As we reviewed in the first part of the book, naughty steps, standing in corners and the use of timers just don't make Time Out a very calming experience. In fact, many children get more worked up and upset when they have to sit alone in Time Out and really do not use this time to reflect on their actions at all. Having the skills to calm down, however, are at the heart of being able to pause, and not melt down when faced with stress, adversity and frustration. Especially as babies transition towards toddlers, then grow into preschoolers and into the elementary age, having the skill to calm down and not melt down is indispensable, not only for the child but for us parents as well.

While the traditional, sit-all-alone element of Time Out doesn't quite help children learn to self-regulate, cool off and reflect, this last connected discipline tool has the potential to do just that.

Why Calm Down Plans Are Helpful

Creating a Calm Down Plan is all about helping your child choose the most helpful ways for them, individually, to calm down and reflect when they need some space. This last tool, the Calm Down Plan, when used properly, positively and in a non-punitive manner can be very helpful to the whole family.

There will be times when taking a Time In together just will not seem possible, you may personally be very agitated and need to calm yourself, or may need to tend to younger children. Additionally, your child may outgrow their willingness to sit with you and would rather be alone for a moment when they feel overwhelmed. This is developmentally expected and healthy, and supporting this need for the child to be alone, yet accepted, is important. Establishing a Calm Down Plan creates the possibility for your child to choose to step away from a difficult situation, and take a moment to calm himself down.

Sometimes children just need to release pent up energy and big, big emotions!

In my family we use a Calm Down bag, a cloth bag that is filled with tinkering toys, a sand timer, a stress ball and other such items. Another possibility is implementing a calm down corner, which is a space dedicated for children to visit when they need to calm down (more specifics on this below). Having a Calm Down strategy works not only to prevent meltdowns, they can also be used when children have become completely unglued. Sometimes children really do need to release pent up energy and big emotions, and having a plan, in the long term, teaches children to recognize when they are feeling overwhelmed, angry, frustrated and in need of a break.

How To Introduce A Calm Down Plan

The key to having a good Calm Down Plan that will actually work is to talk about the plan when things are going well. Introduce the idea of a Calm Down Plan as something that everyone in the house can try and, even better, involve your child in the process of creating his own plan such as choosing materials and suggesting a location. In addition to talking about when and how to use a Calm Down Plan, your child needs to know what is healthy, allowed and expected of them when they feel overwhelmed with strong feelings. Explain that, while it is valid and normal to feel frustration and anger, acting in ways that are hurtful is not acceptable. Your child will need your guidance and help to understand the difference between having big feelings and using destructive behaviors. Tommy's mother worked on helping Tommy learn exactly that difference:

Tommy, at age five, tended to have really big, explosive tantrums shortly after the birth of his sister. His parents explained they would scoop him up and place him in the "naughty corner" when this would happen, except that it wasn't working. In fact, they said, it seemed like each day they needed to use the Time Out corner more and more and Tommy's screams and reactions like kicking the door were getting louder and stronger. In coaching, we talked quite a bit about how the arrival of a sibling can be a big transition. We reviewed ideas like the fact that older children may feel left out or pushed aside. We also agreed that Tommy could benefit from learning some coping skills for when he feels frustrated and how to redirect his aggression. After discussing a few different options, Tanya thought that having a Calm Down Plan for Tommy might work. A few weeks later we reconnected and she shared this: "It's a whole new dynamic around here, and a good one at that. Tommy is loving his Calm Down Corner and tinkering materials. He still gets worked up at times, but when I invite him to walk with me to his calm down spot, he practically runs there, sits and starts ripping sheets of paper into small pieces. Eventually he moves onto the stress ball and then he points to the face pictures to say how he feels. He has a way to tell me he is upset or mad. I can understand him better now, and I swear he knows that. Instead of daily tantrums we are seeing tantrum now maybe once a week now. The Calm Down corner helps us both have a place to go and really take a break instead of losing it, blaming each other, name calling and struggling to be together. It's been a priceless addition to our house."

Calm Down as a Choice, not a Command
Using a Calm Down Plan should be offered as a choice and not a command, otherwise it turns into Time Out all over again. If you see your child is getting wound up, as you have previously talked about the plan, you can direct your child to put his plan into action. "I can see you are getting upset. I think it might be a good time to try your calm down plan. Would you like me to walk with you to the chill-out corner?"

Your child can greatly benefit from watching how you model using a Calm Down Plan as well. Cheryl, a mom to two, shared this story on using a calm down time for herself:

My daughter Melanie felt like resting on her bed instead of helping me sort her own laundry. She wanted nothing to do with my kind requests for help and my patience was getting thin. Really thin! Sensing I was going to get angry at her behavior I knew I needed to get out of there. I told her I was getting aggravated and would be going to my own room to take a five minute calming break. After my break, I realized that Melanie was old enough to do her laundry sorting on her own if she refused my help. I let her know my limits by telling her I would help her then or she could do it on her own at a later time. She chose to do it later, and to my surprise, she actually did it. I was glad I took the time to cool off instead of getting angry.

Setting Up a Calm Down Corner

For many families, a Calm Down Plan involves having a bag, box or corner filled with items that will help the child cope with strong emotions, release tensions and learn to self-regulate.

Here is a list of materials you can consider for a Calm Down space, bag or box:

For smashing, poking or squeezing

- Stress balls
- Play-dough
- Moon sand
- Rice sock
- Pompoms
- Fidget toys

For ripping, cutting, tearing and crumpling

- Old newspaper
- Magazines
- Colorful paper

For Social Emotional Learning

- Pictures of family members with various expressions
- Drawings or images of a range of emotions
- Cards with names of feelings and emotions

For concentrating and calming

- Puzzles
- Lavender pillow
- Rice bottle or Glitter Jar
- Books
- Music player and calming music

Calm Down Plans can also eventually become such a habit that you can use them anywhere and not just at home in a specific corner. For example, my middle son Nicolas at age six was having a bit of a hard time at an amusement park over summer vacation. It was a hot day, we had waited in many lines for rides and a boy cut in front of him in line for a really exciting ride. It was enough to put my son into overwhelm mode and he started to tense up and talk really fast. As I heard "No fair, I can't believe it!" I could tell his frustration and tiredness could potentially turn into a full meltdown. I asked him to follow me and we found a quiet spot behind a wooden gazebo. I took a tinkering toy out of my purse and asked if he would like a few minutes to tinker. While I sat nearby, I gave him space to be mad about what had happened. After a while, he called me over and we hugged. He explained he was really disappointed that after waiting so long, a boy just cut in line and took his spot. The situation really hadn't been fair, but we weren't in a position to "fix it" either. My son was able to feel his frustration, articulate it and then eventually move through it.

Calm down Plans by Age & Stage

TODDLERS (12 MONTHS TO 36 MONTHS)
Toddlers do better with a Time In (see connected discipline tool #1) or a combination of a Time In with calming tools from a Calm Down Plan. Toddlers are not quite able to recognize their own feelings are overwhelming them before it strikes, so it takes a lot of observation and being pro-active to prevent tantrums. Quite honestly, it's often just not possible, and more helpful to simply shift into a mindset of accepting that tantrums are developmentally expected. Toddlers also benefit from emotion coaching in the form of sports casting their feelings,

such as offering gentle words that help them understand why they are so upset. "I see you are very upset/frustrated/sad/mad. I would like to help you calm down." Modeling how you calm down is especially helpful to children in the toddler, as well as preschooler years.

PRE-SCHOOL CHILDREN (36 MONTHS TO 5 YEARS)
Between the ages of three and five years, children that have a good social-emotional vocabulary are much more able to engage in self-calming activities. Aside from modeling how to use a Calm Down Plan, it is also helpful to make a positive effort to not come unglued yourself when your child has strong emotional displays. The preschool years are full of big, potentially explosive moments as children at this age are still learning to regulate their impulses and feel things deeply. This is the age where "I hate you!" may be expressed one minute followed by "I love you forever, and ever and ever!" The calmer you can stay in those moments of big expressions, the more security you can offer to your child. Setting up a routine like using a rice bottle or sitting in a Calm Down zone with a parent nearby is often very helpful.

ELEMENTARY KIDS (5 YEARS TO 10 YEARS)
Between ages five and ten, children tend to respond very well to being in charge of their own calm down plan. Sit together to brainstorm, honor your child's choices, and provide them with the tools (within reason) that they believe will be helpful to them in creating a good "go to" calming plan. Be mindful of not imposing your ideas on this age group, as they much prefer to not be told how to calm down. It's still a good idea to offer guidance though and help them to realize when taking a moment to cool off is called for. Children at this stage also need to feel validated and understood, so whenever possible, create the opportunity for your child to talk to you about what they are feeling, thinking and deciding after they have calmed down. Just nodding, and being present, without offering to "fix" their situation is usually sufficient and more helpful at this age, and will create a dynamic of trust and openness. This is also an age

where gradually offering the child more space to reflect and process feelings alone will be appropriate.

Calm Down corners and plans will not always prevent meltdowns, but they can be a positive way to direct emotional overwhelm and energy into a more connected, shame-free practice that honors, validates and accepts our children.

Bonus Tool: Reconnecting After a Disconnect

Parenting is a really tough job and it's pretty much impossible to do it perfectly. These tools alone will not work without patience, a sense of humor, consistency, flexibility and hard work. No matter what parenting book or advice you choose to follow, you may, at some point, fall back into some kind of parenting decision you later regret. Perhaps in a moment of frustration or anger you threaten or use a punitive consequence. Maybe regardless of your very best intentions you find yourself yelling, "That's it – Get into Time Out!"

Don't lose faith in connected discipline. Sometimes, no matter how calm, connected and peaceful we intend to be...we react. Learning to recover when we make a mistake really does help restore connection, models really important skills to our children and helps things shift back into a calmer, positive, connected place.

It takes just 3 steps towards recovering from a disconnected moment:

Rewind: Acknowledge that you have said or done something hurtful or rude.

What you say to yourself may sound like: "I'm at the end of my rope, I need to stop and start over"

Repair: Apologize for not only what you said, but also how you did it.

What you say to your child may sound like: "I yelled and sent you to time out, which wasn't a good way to tell you want I really wanted. I am sorry for yelling. I love you."

Replay: Try again, this time responding with kindness and the intent to connect to your child.

What you say next may sound like: "I'd like to work together. Let's start over." And then you can pick a tool like problem solving, asking questions or limited choices to move forward.

As individuals, we are imperfect and affected by our own stressors and life stories. I can assure you, your children don't expect perfection and they do genuinely love you for you. After working with so many parents, I can say quite honestly, it's not unusual for parents to feel annoyed, overwhelmed, bothered or even down right angry with their children. Maybe it is undone chores, skipped naps, the spills, the tears, the teasing...the car will not start, the laundry is piling up, the toilet clogged, the dog barfed, the phone rang again and dinner is about to burn... Life is busy, we have high expectations, worries, plans and well...there are also countless amazing moments; when siblings help each other, when your child offers you that big, sweet grin in the morning, when your child tells their first joke, offers to help you with cooking, hugs you with so much love you think being a parent is the most amazing thing ever... Be kind to yourself, take breaks when you can, forgive your own mistakes.

Even if we can't parent in the most nurturing ways all the time, the more often we can, the more our children get what they need, the better they will be able to weather the times when we parent in less nurturing ways. –Pam Leo.

Children have a natural desire to learn and to follow those they trust and love, so cherish that responsibility, forgive your own shortcomings with the same love and empathy you would extend to your child. Show up, be present and have the courage to try again when needed. Don't forget to attend to your own needs for resting, recharging and pursuing your own interests. That kind of attitude will model to your child more skills than any book, parenting method or alternative to time out ever could.

Part Three

Children's Story Books
Parenting Books & Pages
Acknowledgements
About the Author

Recommended Resources

Children's Story Books for Social-Emotional Learning

Each book in this list was chosen because they offer great starting points to discuss important topics like overcoming challenges, naming emotions and feelings, understanding conflict, navigating friendships and paying attention to each other's needs. The age recommendation is just a general guideline.

Alexander and the Terrible, Horrible, No Good, Very Bad Day by Judith Viorst (Ages 4-8)

Andrew's Angry Words by Dorothea Lackner (Ages 4-8)

Bootsie Barker Bites by Barbara Bottner (Ages 4-8)

The Chocolate Covered Cookie Tantrum by Deborah Blementhal (Ages 5-8)

How I Feel Frustrated by Marcia Leonard (Ages 3-8)

How I Feel Angry by Marcia Leonard (Ages 2-6)

Llama Llama Mad at Mama by Anna Dewdney (Ages 2-5)

Sometimes I'm Bombaloo by Rachel Vail (Ages 3-8)

That Makes Me Mad! by Steven Kroll (Ages 4-8)

Feeling Happy by Ellen Weiss (Ages infants -3)

Glad Monster, Sad Monster by Ed Emberley & Anne Miranda (Ages infant-5)

I Love You All Day Long by Francesca Rusackas (Ages 3-5)

Enemy Pie by Derek Munson (Ages 5-9)

The Grouchy Ladybug by Eric Carle (Ages 1-6)

The Rain Came Down by David Shannon (Ages 4-8)

When I'm Angry by Jane Aaron (Ages 3-7)

When I'm Feeling Angry by Trace Moroney (Ages 2-5)

When I Feel Angry by Cornelia Maude Spelman (Ages 5-7)

When Sophie Gets Angry – Really, Really Angry by Molly G (Ages 4-8)

Creepy Things are Scaring Me by Jerome and Jarrett Pumphrey (Ages 4-8)

Franklin in The Dark by Paulette Bourgeois & Brenda Clark (Ages 5-8)

It's Okay to Be Different by Todd Parr (Ages 3-8)

How I Feel Scared by Marcia Leonard (Ages 2-6)

I Am Not Going to School Today by Robie H. Harris (Ages 4-8)

No Such Thing by Jackie French Koller (Ages 5-8)

Today I Feel Silly & Other Moods That Make My Day by Jamie Lee (Ages 3-8)

Sam's First Day by David Mills & Lizzie Finlay (Ages 3-7)

Sheila Rae, the Brave, by Kevin Henkes (Ages 5-8)

Wemberly Worried by Kevin Henkes (Ages 5-8)

When I'm Feeling Scared by Trace Moroney (Ages 2-5)

When I Feel Scared by Cornelia Maude Spelman (Ages 5-7)

Bear Feels Sick by Karma Wilson and Jane Chapman (Ages 3-5)

Can You Tell How Someone Feels by Nita Everly (ages 3-6)

Understand and Care by Cheri Meiners (Ages 3-6)

When I Care about Others by Cornelia Maude Spelman (Ages 5+)

How I Feel Sad by Marcia Leonard (Ages 2-6)

Hurty Feelings by Helen Lester (Ages 5-8)

Knuffle Bunny by Mo Willems (Ages 3-6)

Sometimes I Feel Awful by Joan Singleton Prestine (Ages 5-8)

The Very Lonely Firefly by Eric Carle (Ages 4-7)

Peekaboo Morning by Rachel Isadora (Ages 2-5)

When I Feel Happy by Marcia Leonard (Ages 2-6)

"What Went Right Today?" by Joan Buzick and Lindy Judd (Ages 3 – 8)

Don't Let the Pigeon Drive the Bus by Mo Willems (Ages 2-7)

Don't Let the Pigeon Stay Up Late! by Mo Willems (Ages 2-7)

I Did It, I'm Sorry by Caralyn Buehner (Ages 5-8)

It Wasn't My Fault by Helen Lester (Ages 4-7)

Talk and Work it Out by Cheri Meiners (Ages 4-8)

Full, Full, Full of Love by Trish Cooke (Ages 4-6)

Don't Forget I Love You by Mariam Moss (Ages 2-7)

Guess How Much I Love You By Sam McBratney (Ages infant-5)

Owl Babies by Martin Waddell (Ages 3-7)

How Do I Love You? by P.K. Hallinan (Ages infant-5)

Counting Kisses by Karen Katz (Ages infant-5)

The Fall of Freddie the Leaf by Leo Buscaglia (Ages 5-adult)

Goodbye Mousie by Robert Harris (Ages 3-8)

I Create My World by Connie Bowen (All Ages)

I Believe in Me by Connie Bowen (All Ages)

The Little Book of Harmony by Kerry Spina (All Ages)

Parenting Books
The following books support parenting practices that are aligned with a connected, positive approach to parenting. This is not a complete list, but contains some of my most often recommended books for parents.

Connection Parenting: Parenting Through Connection Instead of Coercion, Through Love Instead of Fear, 2nd Edition Paperback by Pam Leo

Genius in Every Child: Encouraging Character, Curiosity, and Creativity in Children by Rick Ackerly

How to Talk So Kids Will Listen and Listen So Kids Will Talk, by Adele Faber and Elaine Mazlish

When Your Kids Push Your Buttons: And What You Can Do About It. By Bonnie Harris

Parenting From the Inside Out
By Daniel J. Siegel MD, Mary Hartzell

The Explosive Child: A New Approach for Understanding and Parenting Easily Frustrated, Chronically Inflexible Children
By Ross W., PhD Greene

Raising An Emotionally Intelligent Child: The Heart of Parenting
By Ph.D. John Gottman, Joan Declaire

Playful Parenting
By Lawrence J. Cohen

Unconditional Parenting: Moving from Rewards and Punishments to Love and Reason
By Alfie Kohn

The Whole-Brain Child: 12 Revolutionary Strategies to Nurture Your Child's Developing Mind
By Daniel J. Siegel, Tina Payne Bryson

Peaceful Parent, Happy Kids: How to Stop Yelling and Start Connecting
By Dr. Laura Markham

Positive Discipline A-Z: 1001 Solutions to Everyday Parenting Problems (Positive Discipline Library)
By Jane Nelsen Ed.D., Lynn Lott, H. Stephen Glenn

Positive Parenting in Action: The How-To Guide for Putting Positive Parenting Principles into Action in Early Childhood
By Laura Ling, Rebecca Eanes

Whispers Through Time: Communication Through the Ages and Stages of Childhood (A Little Hearts Handbook)
By L.R. Knost

Attached at the Heart: Eight Proven Parenting Principles for Raising Connected and Compassionate Children
By Barbara Nicholson, Lysa Parker

Daring Greatly: How the Courage to Be Vulnerable Transforms the Way We Live, Love, Parent, and Lead
By Brene Brown

Encouraging Words for Kids
By Kelly Bartlett

Helping Young Children Flourish
By Aletha Jauch Solter

Raising Our Children, Raising Ourselves: Transforming parent-child relationships from reaction and struggle to freedom, power and joy
by Naomi Aldort

Parent Effectiveness Training by Dr. Thomas Gordon

References

1 Kostewicz, Douglas E.A (2010) Review of Timeout Ribbons Behavior Analyst Today, v11 n2 p95-104

2 Obsuth, I., Hennighausen, K., Brumariu, L. E. and Lyons-Ruth, K. (2014), Disorganized Behavior in Adolescent–Parent Interaction: Relations to Attachment State of Mind, Partner Abuse, and Psychopathology. Child Development, 85: 370–387.

3 George W. Holden, Paul A. Williamson, Grant W. O. Holland. (2014) Eavesdropping on the family: A pilot investigation of corporal punishment in the home. Journal of Family Psychology.

4 Gershoff, E. T., & Bitensky, S. H. (2007). The case against corporal punishment of children: Converging evidence from social science research and international human rights law and implications for U.S. public policy. Psychology, Public Policy, And Law, 13(4), 231-272. doi:10.1037/1076-8971.13.4.231

5 Kaminski JW, Valle LA, Filene JH, Boyle CL. (2008) A meta-analytic review of components associated with parent training program effectiveness. Journal of Abnormal Child Psychology; 26:567–89.

6 Mathis, Erin; Bierman, Karen (2012), Child Emotion Regulation and Attentional Control in Pre-Kindergarten: Associations with Parental Stress, Parenting Practices, and Parent-Child Interaction Quality Society for Research on Educational Effectiveness

7 Obsuth, I., Hennighausen, K., Brumariu, L. E. and Lyons-Ruth, K. (2014), Disorganized Behavior in Adolescent–Parent Interaction: Relations to Attachment State of Mind, Partner Abuse, and Psychopathology. Child Development, 85: 370–387.

8 Smith, Anne B. (2004) How Do Infants and Toddlers Learn the Rules? Family Discipline and Young Children International Journal of Early Childhood, v36 n2 p27-42

9 Berk, L. E., Mann, T.D., & Ogan, A.T. (2006). Make-Believe play: Wellspring for development of self-regulation. In D. Singer, R.M. Golinkoff, & Hirsh-Pasek (Eds.), Play =Learning: How play motivates and enhances children's cognitive and social-emotional growth. New York, NY: Oxford University Press.

10 Campbell, Susan (1995) Behavior Problems in Preschool Children: A Review of Recent Research. J. Child Psychol Psychiat. 36(1):113-149

11 Halford, W. K., & Petch, J. (2010). Couple psychoeducation for new parents: Observed and potential effects on parenting. Clinical Child and Family Psychology Review, 13, 164-180. doi: 10.1007/s 10567-0100066-z

12 Halford, W. K" Petch, J., & Creedy, D. K. (2010). Promoting a positive transition to parenthood: A randomized clinical trial of couple relationship education. Prevention Science, II, 89-100. doi: 10.1007/s 11121009-0152-y

Acknowledgements

This book would not have been possible without my children, who inspire me daily to develop and practice the very tools I have written about. I would also like to thank my parents and sisters for being an incredible source of support and love. A heartfelt thank you to Beth Gaylor of Beginning Years Family Network for inspiring me to become a parenting educator. Tiziana Marcon for your continued mentorship. Anne Jones for her fabulous editing and continued friendship and Kerry Spina of Kids in Harmony for invaluable feedback and support. A special thank you to my husband not only for general support but also for assuming all laundry duties so I could get this project finished.

I would also like to extend a very special thank you to the amazing parenting experts, writers and educators that I continue to learn from, and share work with. Alice Hanscam of Denali Parent Coaching, Amy Phoenix of Presence Parenting, Casey O'Roarty of Joyful Courage, Kelly Bartlett of Parenting From Scratch, Genevieve Simperingham of the Peaceful Parenting Institute, Andrea Nair of Connect Four Parenting, Laura Markham of Aha!Parenting, Rick Ackerly of The Genius in Every Child, Andy Smithson of Tru Parenting, Marilyn-Price Mitchell of Roots of Action, Becky Eanes of Positive-Parents.org, Gena Kirby, of Progressive Parenting Radio, Amy Miller McCready of Positive Parenting Solutions, Debbie Morrison Zeichner, LCSW, Parent Coach, Alanna McGinn of Good Night Sleep Site, and Jane Nelson of the Positive Discipline Series.

Lastly, a very special thank you to all the parents and children that have kindly shared their personal stories, struggles and successes to be included in this book

About the Author

Ariadne Brill is a parenting educator, mother to three children and the founder of the Positive Parenting Connection. In addition to writing and presenting workshops on parenting topics, she facilitates parent-child playgroups for toddlers and preschoolers for various community organizations focusing on healthy attachment and development through play, music and movement. She has a B.S. in Communication and Creative Expression from James Madison University and is a certified Positive Discipline Parenting Educator through the Positive Discipline Association. In continuing her education, she has completed several graduate courses in psychology, child development, child psychology, family violence prevention and family counseling. Her writings on alternatives to Time Out, avoiding power struggles and positive parenting have been published in several parenting magazines, newsletters and websites around the world.

Connect with Ariadne
Email
info@parentcoa.ch

Web
Positive Parenting Connection
http://positiveparentingconnection.net

Social Media
https://twitter.com/positive_parent
http://www.pinterest.com/ppconnection/

Positive Parenting Page on Facebook
http://www.facebook.com/positiveparentingconnection

Join our Positive Parenting Questions & Answers Forum
https://www.facebook.com/groups/parentsSHARE/

20330078R00060

Printed in Great Britain
by Amazon